Praise for *Paul an*

We can learn so much from the lives of the earliest
ordinary people who, obedient to God's leading, p
circles the globe. In *Paul and His Team*, Ryan Lokk
hearts and actions of these pioneering believers, yi
can be salt and light in a challenging world.

RICHARD STEARNS
President of World Vision U.S. and author of *The Hole in Our Gospel*

Build bridges, be voices of reconciliation, seek common ground, stay focused on your
mission as Christ's ambassadors: *Paul and His Team* offers practical advice to advance the
gospel, rooted in solid biblical teaching for both pastors and lay leaders. Helpful questions
at the end of each chapter make this an excellent group study book.

LYNN COHICK
New Testament department chair at Wheaton College

Ryan takes a powerful yet practical look at not just the apostle Paul, but at Paul's team, as
it applies to leading in the church. If you are a leader, the people and team you build are
critical to moving the mission of the church forward. In *Paul and His Team*, Ryan pulls out
important insight on church leadership and influence.

CAREY NIEUWHOF
Founding Pastor, Connexus Church

In a day when we only think about the "super leaders" in the big lights, Lokkesmoe
insightfully highlights the whole cast of lesser known men and women who supported
Paul's apostolic mission. In the process we learn valuable lessons about leadership, conflict
resolution, and true kingdom collaboration. This book quietly turns most leadership books
on their heads, demonstrating the real work of God through the lives of ordinary, flawed
people who offer their disparate gifts to the Master. I heartily recommend it.

TIMOTHY C. TENNENT
President and Professor of World Christianity, Asbury Theological Seminary

Ryan Lokkesmoe explores the real-life implications of how the body of Christ is supposed
to work together to fulfill the Great Commission. In a day and age where there is far too
much emphasis upon upfront leaders and not enough on the power of a team, Ryan offers
a helpful contribution that is both accessible and scholarly. If you are a leader or part of a
leadership team, you will find his insights helpful.

LARRY OSBORNE
Pastor and Author, North Coast Church

In *Paul and His Team*, Ryan Lokkesmoe provides an accessible guide to the leadership
example of Paul that will help pastors and lay leaders better steward the responsibility God
has given them.

MICHAEL WEAR
Author of *Reclaiming Hope: Lessons Learned in the Obama White House About the Future of
Faith in America*

Looking for a new twist on effective leadership? This may be just what you're looking for! In contrast to the "latest and greatest" leadership theories, Ryan Lokkesmoe leads us back to the early church for in-depth perspective on the leadership strategy of the apostle Paul. Highly recommended!

JOE STOWELL
President, Cornerstone University, Grand Rapids, MI

I strongly believe that great leadership is a team sport. In *Paul and His Team*, Ryan masterfully gives us practical leadership applications from his thorough research into the team that supported the apostle Paul's ministry. Every leadership team should study and implement the lessons from this book!

CHRIS SURRATT
Discipleship and Small Group Specialist, LifeWay Christian Resources
Author of *Small Groups for the Rest of Us*

Paul and His Team is a practical and accessible book that dives into the leadership principles of first-century ministers, then applies them to life and ministry in the twenty-first century. The way it is organized, from building bridges with nonbelievers and walking them through baby steps, all the way to mature Christian faith and training the next generation of leaders, is especially helpful.

KARL VATERS
Pastor, author, and blogger (NewSmallChurch.com)

This outstanding gem of a book is an honest and cutting-edge guide to becoming winsome, gracious, and effective on- and off-stage leaders in our challenging new cultural context. It is a marvelous treasure trove of fresh, biblical, and hard-hitting insights. The apostle Paul urged believers to imitate him and his team, and Ryan Lokkesmoe breaks down for us how to do this in the twenty-first century. I heartily recommend this powerfully relevant book.

COLIN R. NICHOLL
Director, Biblical Research Ministries, Northern Ireland
Author, *The Great Christ Comet: Revealing the True Star of Bethlehem*

Popular-level leadership manuals abound. Many Christian manuals exist as well, often prooftexting principles initially derived from sources other than the Bible. Ryan Lokkesmoe carefully studies Paul and his coworkers, fully abreast of the highest levels of scholarship, and discovers principles that really are in Scripture! But he wears his learning lightly and writes with the heart of the church planter that he currently is. Easy to read and highly recommended.

CRAIG L. BLOMBERG
Distinguished Professor of New Testament, Denver Seminary

Viewing leadership as Christ-centered influence, Ryan Lokkesmoe insightfully lays out the principles employed by Paul and his ministry cohorts. With solid biblical scholarship and practical application to Christian leadership, Ryan has provided a significant, readable gift to the church. This book is much richer than the trendy "how-to" leadership books currently on the market. Highly recommended for pastors and lay leaders!

DENNIS P. HOLLINGER
President & Colman M. Mockler Distinguished Professor of Christian Ethics at Gordon-Conwell Theological Seminary

PAUL

AND HIS

TEAM

WHAT THE EARLY CHURCH CAN TEACH US ABOUT LEADERSHIP AND INFLUENCE

RYAN LOKKESMOE, PhD

MOODY PUBLISHERS

CHICAGO

Unless otherwise indicated, Scripture quotations are from the ESV® Bible (The Holy Bible, English Standard Version®), copyright © 2001 by Crossway, a publishing ministry of Good News Publishers. Used by permission. All rights reserved.

Scripture quotations marked NIV are taken from the Holy Bible, New International Version®, NIV®. Copyright © 1973, 1978, 1984, 2011 by Biblica, Inc.™ Used by permission of Zondervan. All rights reserved worldwide. www.zondervan.com. The "NIV" and "New International Version" are trademarks registered in the United States Patent and Trademark Office by Biblica, Inc.™

Published in association with Literary Agent Janet Kobobel Grant of Books & Such Literary Management, 5926 Sunhawk Dr., Santa Rosa, CA 95409.

Emphasis in Scripture has been added.

Edited by Matthew Boffey
Author photo: Danielle Chisler / Chisler Photography
Interior design: Erik M. Peterson
Cover design: Faceout Studios
Cover image texture copyright © 2017 by Apostrophe / Shutterstock (279241004). All rights reserved.

Library of Congress Cataloging-in-Publication Data

Names: Lokkesmoe, Ryan, author.
Title: Paul and his team : what the early church can teach us about
  leadership and influence / by Ryan Lokkesmoe, PhD.
Description: Chicago : Moody Publishers, 2017. | Includes bibliographical
  references.
Identifiers: LCCN 2017027184 (print) | LCCN 2017034389 (ebook) | ISBN
  9780802495525 | ISBN 9780802415646
Subjects: LCSH: Paul, the Apostle, Saint--Influence. | Paul, the Apostle,
  Saint--Friends and associates. | Christian leadership. | Church
  history--Primitive and early church, ca. 30-600.
Classification: LCC BS2506.3 (ebook) | LCC BS2506.3 .L65 2017 (print) | DDC
  225.9/2--dc23
LC record available at https://lccn.loc.gov/2017027184

We hope you enjoy this book from Moody Publishers. Our goal is to provide high-quality, thought-provoking books and products that connect truth to your real needs and challenges. For more information on other books and products written and produced from a biblical perspective, go to www.moodypublishers.com or write to:

Moody Publishers
820 N. LaSalle Boulevard
Chicago, IL 60610

1 3 5 7 9 10 8 6 4 2

For Mom, Dad, Grandma, Grandpa, Pete Briscoe,
Mark Saunders, and Tom Eichem:
the exceptional team that God
assembled for my spiritual upbringing.

CONTENTS

FOREWORD

Erastus. Rufus. Gaius. Phoebe. Priscilla. Olympas. Aquila. These names may not mean anything to us, but they meant the world to Paul.

Paul's letter to the church in Rome was his most theological and philosophical work to that point, and it has become esteemed as the most systematic, categorical, and chronological declaration of faith in the entire New Testament. As he wrapped up his letter in a section we refer to as Romans 16, Paul's grand conclusion consisted of a list of almost three dozen names. After he put the period on his statement of faith, he let the credits roll. These were the people who had shaped him and formed him, people who had invested in him, people who had taken a risk on him, people who had been crazy enough to join him. The list included the people who had learned from him, stepped up to continue the legacy he had passed to them, and committed to making disciples of the next generation. They were his mentors and mentees, his disciples, his spiritual family, and his team. Paul recognized that even his theology could not be developed in a vacuum and his ministry could not be fulfilled alone.

In a sense, he was declaring, "I can't tell my story of faith without mentioning these names."

Paul is credited with starting churches in Philippi, Corinth, and Crete, but they would not have thrived without the leadership of people like Lydia, Aquila, Priscilla, Erastus, Epaphroditus, Timothy, Titus, and an unnamed Philippian jailer. Paul is named as the author of about half of the books in the New Testament, but men like Sosthenes, Silas, and Timothy were also contributors. Paul's may be the name everyone knows, but completing his gospel mission required a team.

Now Ryan Lokkesmoe has given us a fresh window into Paul's leadership and influence, focusing on the team he recruited, developed, entrusted, and unleashed. While Ryan has the academic credentials to give us a deeply theological understanding of the life and ministry of Paul, this book is not merely theoretical. Ryan has not simply studied these topics in the classroom; he is also a practitioner who has learned these valuable lessons in the trenches of real-life ministry. While serving as a Small Groups Pastor at a multisite church, he learned the value of a team. More recently, as he has planted and now pastors a church, he recognizes that his influence will only grow when he develops those around him.

One of the most important jobs of a leader is to develop an effective team, which involves building, growing, entrusting, and unleashing them. This is not easy. It takes character, humility, patience, perseverance, and confidence. It requires thick skin and a soft heart. *Paul and His Team* doesn't give formulas, lists, or step-by-step instructions for establishing great teams. Instead, Ryan reveals how specific New Testament situations and circumstances can help us think more deeply, critically, and creatively about who we are as a leader, the individuals on our teams, how we work together, and why we make the decisions we do. Most importantly, you will learn from one of the first ministry teams how to impact your world with the gospel.

If you had a Romans 16 list, what names would be on it? Who has played a critical role in supporting your calling or ministry? And whose list would your name be on? Who can't tell their story of faith without mentioning your name? How are you loving these people, challenging them, believing in them, confronting them, and entrusting leadership to them? The value of your leadership and influence is directly proportional to the strength of the team you lead.

HEATHER ZEMPEL

Author of *Amazed and Confused* and *Community Is Messy*

Finding Our Future in the Past

If you are reading these words, God has given you many gifts: a beating heart, a functioning brain, breath in your lungs, many years' worth of food and water, eyesight, and literacy—just to name a few. God has given all of us gifts. Some are physical like a roof over our heads in a hailstorm. Others are less tangible but still observable, like the musical talent of a virtuoso classical guitarist. All God's gifts, whatever form they take, come with the joy and responsibility of being used for His glory.

Influence is a gift that God has given all of us, and it's one that we easily neglect. We all have some sort of influence over someone else: our children, employees, friends, neighbors, coworkers, followers on social media, and so on. Whether it's one person or a thousand, there is *someone* out there looking to us as an example in some way. Sometimes that influence is formalized into a visible leadership role or occupation. But even if we don't view ourselves as leaders or hold some sort of leadership title, we all have influence and the accompanying charge to honor the Lord in how we use it.

If you are a Christian, then you are the beneficiary of two thousand years' worth of ongoing, overlapping influence. The gospel was propelled through the generations by the Holy Spirit, working through all sorts of relationships and styles of influence. To glimpse the beautiful spectrum of influence that has moved through the centuries since the time of Christ, we need only look at a tiny slice of that history as an example.

Elizabeth grew up in New England, and faith was not a part of her life at all. Her father would angrily slam the door in the face of traveling evangelists when they came by the house. Elizabeth first heard the gospel as a teenager when she was invited to a church event by a friend named Ginnie. She placed her trust in Christ that day. In the early days of her faith, Elizabeth had the opportunity to hear Billy Graham speak when he was just getting started. His passionate words helped reinforce the gospel in her heart, and she spent the rest of her life following Christ.

In the early 1950s, Elizabeth enrolled at Nyack College in New York, where she met a man named Bob who was studying to become a pastor. The school assigned seating at tables in the cafeteria, and Bob ended up at Elizabeth's table. Bob was from a Norwegian family and grew up in the Lutheran tradition. He learned about Jesus at a young age and placed his trust in Christ at a Salvation Army meeting in Minnesota when he was seven years old.

Bob and Elizabeth were married in 1952 and spent their lives in ministry afterwards. They are my grandparents.

Bob and Elizabeth had a daughter and then a son—my dad. He learned about Jesus from my grandparents and became a Christian at a young age. A couple of decades later he met my mom and took her to a Billy Graham crusade at San Jose State University in 1981, where she placed her faith in Christ. I was born in 1982, and because of their influence my brother and I met Jesus when we were young. Through the ministry of several great local churches over the years, I grew in my faith, which really took root when I was in high school. My wife's family has an equally rich spiritual history, and as parents we are now seeking the Lord's guidance on raising our two young children.

What stands out to me about this brief history is the *variety* of influences God used to shape the spiritual life of my family: friendships, family relationships, local churches, pastors, parachurch organizations, and evangelistic events. I'm sure there are many other leaders, books, and experiences that played a role as well. And that's just my family. If God enabled us to zoom out and comprehend all the millions of relationships and interactions that have fueled the growth of the church over the last two thousand years, we would be amazed by the assortment of influence and leadership styles that were at work.

God has enabled each of us to play our part in this story—to apply the influence He has given us in ways big and small, in grand efforts and mundane interactions. How will we use that influence? How will we lead? How would someone three generations from now describe our role in their faith story?

Over the years I've sometimes wondered how it's even possible that I'm a Christian. How was I in a position to be influenced by other Christians? How is it possible that the church survived as long as it has and carried the gospel across so many geographical, cultural, and language barriers? I have thought about this a lot because I spent the majority of my education studying the historical context of the New Testament. I'm astounded by the number of hurdles that the early church faced.

Many Jews viewed Christians as heretics. Greeks and Romans thought they were strange. Imperial officials believed they were disloyal. Christians were generally poor, marginalized people. Few "qualified" leaders were available to shepherd the church in the early days, and false teachers were a constant source of discord and division. From an earthly perspective, the first-century Christians had few advantages.

But in spite of these challenges, the church grew like wildfire. Within one generation, Christianity went from a small, relatively obscure community of believers on the fringe of the Roman Empire to a movement that spanned the Mediterranean.

The only explanation for this growth is that God made it happen. That's how the church survived its infancy and continued to flourish for twenty centuries, eventually reaching my family tree. I'm convinced that if the growth of Christianity were dependent on human effort it would have evaporated long ago in the face of external social pressures and internal leadership challenges. In the book of Acts, Luke states that the Holy Spirit drove the growth of the church: "So the church throughout all Judea and Galilee and Samaria had peace and was being built up. And walking in the fear of the Lord and in the comfort of the Holy Spirit, it multiplied" (Acts 9:31).

The apostle Paul also acknowledged this reality. When

people were comparing his leadership to that of Apollos (another well-known early-Christian leader), Paul said, "I planted, Apollos watered, but God gave the growth" (1 Cor. 3:6). I'm not sure there is a more concise expression of Christian leadership in the Bible. God grows His church, but He allows us to contribute to that process through the gifts and influence He has given us. That's how it worked in the early church, that's how it works today, and that's how it has worked in every century in between.

In the first century, Paul assembled and mobilized a team of gifted leaders who worked together for the common purpose of sharing Christ with the world. We mainly hear about Paul, but he operated within a network of teammates who were influencing communities all around the Roman world. Who were these members of Paul's team, and what were the challenges they faced? How did their solutions and failures impact their ministry, and what can we learn from their experiences?

Before we explore those questions, I want to be clear that this book is not just for ministry professionals. While on the surface the activities of Paul's team most closely resemble the work of full-time pastors, it would be a serious error to conclude that the lessons we learn from them are only meant to be applied in professional ministry circles. Understanding the spiritual outlook and organizational temperament of Paul's team provides wisdom and inspiration for anyone who wants to be a more effective influencer for Christ—whatever your context might be. Parents, teachers, supervisors, employees, coaches, students, volunteers, law enforcement officers, military personnel, church leaders, neighbors, grandparents, friends, siblings—whatever hat you happen to wear—if you have any amount of influence on anyone else (which you do), this book is for you.

The leadership lessons of Paul and his team have always been available to us, but they're sort of hiding in plain sight, camouflaged throughout the New Testament. They are not easily observable because they are obscured by the historical gap between their world and ours. Some of the story is laid out fairly clearly in the book of Acts, but a lot of it is scattered in fragments throughout Paul's letters. It's a task to gather it all together and see it as a unified whole—a cohesive story of Christ-centered leadership.

That is my aim: to gather together that fragmentary evidence and assemble a vivid picture of how Paul's team operated within the first-century church environment. You will find motivation in their example. You will be encouraged by the way they trusted God in the face of adversity. And you will find yourself inspired by the timeless, Christlike qualities they exemplified.

This book is not a step-by-step guide to effective leadership. Instead, think of it as a collection of case studies from Paul's ministry that illustrate certain principles—how we are to influence the world around us. Many leadership books address the mechanics of leadership and primarily focus on *what* and *how* questions. This book will be more concerned with *who* and *why* questions. Who are we as influencers, and why do we lead the way we do?

In the pages that follow, you'll meet Paul's team—valuable players like Mark, Barnabas, Silas, Luke, Priscilla, Aquila, Erastus, Philemon, Onesimus, Tychicus, Epaphras, Titus, and Timothy.[1] Some of these names might be familiar to you, but if you're like me, for a long time I had no clue what these people did or what roles they played on Paul's team. They were just names. As we will see, they each brought their unique gifts, personalities, and experiences to the table and made invaluable contributions to the cause of Christ.

In this book, we will observe Paul's team in action, working in concert to apply timeless, Christ-centered leadership principles like finding common ground, maintaining relationships in the midst of discord, empowering behind-the-scenes leaders, fighting the battles that really matter, working for unity, relentlessly pursuing reconciliation, and relying on God in the face of adversity.

Along the way, you'll also get an overview of the New Testament world and a closer look at Paul, though it will not be a comprehensive introduction to his ministry. The leadership lessons in this book will roughly follow the chronology of Paul's career in ministry, so you'll gain a basic historical framework for understanding much of the New Testament.

In observing Paul's team, we will see a unique form of influence at work. It's crucial that we don't miss the significance of this. We will see qualities like humility, self-sacrifice, and radical grace at work. This stands in stark contrast to much of the leadership culture today, which often has a strident, boastful tone to it—even in Christian circles.

That sort of tone might make sense in the competitive corporate sector or the world of athletics, but we have to be careful about wholeheartedly embracing secular leadership mentalities within the church. Strategies are one thing, and they can be helpful in certain circumstances, but we must be clear-eyed about the fact that they are often born out of mindsets that are at odds with the biblical view of leadership.

The church is like no other organization. It is meant to be a unified, non-competitive entity—described metaphorically in the New Testament as a body or a temple (Rom. 12:4ff; 1 Cor. 12:12ff; Eph. 2:19ff; 4:4, 25; Col. 3:15). God gets all the credit for any growth that occurs. That should affect the way we view ourselves as influencers, the way we talk about our leadership, and the way we lead our teams.

Does God want us to be our best? Yes! But not *the best* in a comparative sense. The church is not a competition. Does He want us to take His church to the next level? Of course! But only in the way that He wants us to and in His timing. Does God want us to "win"? Definitely! But not in the competitive or argumentative sense. He wants us to win hearts for Christ and change the world around us.

We can't forget that the kingdom of God reverses so many aspects of success. Jesus served His disciples. He washed their feet. When His disciples began to posture and compare their leadership prowess, He reprimanded them by saying that leaders must view themselves as servants (Mark 10:35–45). The first will be last. These are notions that are uniquely Christian, and therefore our leadership within the church should always have that distinctive tone and posture when compared to any other leadership context.

We will see that sort of Christian leadership on display. We will observe Paul and his team responding to challenges in ways that are distinctly Christian, with attitudes and strategies that would not be considered winning in other environments. In some cases we can do exactly as Paul and his team did. In other instances we cannot do as they did because of the difference in cultural context, but we can still *act* as they acted. We can adopt their leadership temperament. We can embrace their outlook as Christian influencers. We can prioritize their priorities. We can emulate the deeper character of their ministry and allow it to shape our actions today as it shaped theirs.

We must learn the lessons of Paul's team because even though they were living in a different time in history, many of the challenges they faced are surprisingly similar to obstacles we encounter today. We need to learn these lessons so that the more painful chapters of church history do not needlessly reoccur. When it comes to leadership in the church today, we have to look back in order to effectively look forward.

A couple of necessary qualifications before I continue. First, while I hold a PhD in New Testament, this book is not exactly an academic work.[2] I will not be engaging in the nuanced discussions of New Testament scholarship or substantively interacting with differing scholarly viewpoints on Paul's ministry, as is standard practice in academic writing. This book is written with one foot in academia, and one foot in the world of day-to-day ministry. I will confine my comments about Paul and his ministry to the more generally accepted scholarly views that have been held for some time. I will leave the more granular biblical and theological explorations to others. There are plenty of excellent volumes on Paul's ministry that address those issues. There will be moments in this book, however, when I will turn up the volume on the academic side of things in order to explain something. At other times, my scholarly voice will fade to the background and I will speak more plainly as a husband and father who works in pastoral ministry.

Second, when I use the words *leader* or *leadership*, I am not referring only to those who hold formalized ministry positions. I will generally use the terms *leadership* and *influence* interchangeably, but I won't continually qualify that throughout the book.

I would like to bring this introduction to a close on a note of transparency. As I write these words, I am six weeks into pastoring a new church plant that required over a year of intense preparation. Launching Real Hope Community Church has been the most emotionally draining and spiritually rewarding leadership maneuver I've ever been a part of, and God has taught me a lot of lessons that I'm sure I'll take with me for the rest of my days.

If I learned anything through the process of launching Real Hope, I realized the seemingly obvious fact that every church that has ever existed has been started by someone— and not just someone, a *group* of someones. For us, that group was the Real Hope launch team, and our church would not exist without their commitment to the cause of Christ. We also had the financial, practical, and spiritual support of a broader network that included friends, family members, other churches, and the church-planting organization ARC (Association of Related Churches). We were overwhelmed by the flood of encouragement and support we received in the months leading up to our launch. Now I find that when I read Paul's letters and he rhapsodizes about his friends and coworkers in ministry, I have a new understanding for the deep affection he had for them.

Why am I telling you this? Because I do not want you to read the words in this book and hear my voice as someone who thinks they have arrived as a leader. If anything, I'm more aware than ever of how much more I have to learn. I am asking that God would cement in my heart the principles that we will explore together in this book. Some of them come more easily to me than others, and I'm sure you'll find the same to be true for you.

I am not a perfect leader, and neither are you. Let's accept that reality, and ask the Holy Spirit to teach all of us through the example of Paul and his team. It's my prayer that God would use this book in some way to help you in your journey as an influencer.

Now, let's look together through the telescopic lens of history and observe Paul's team at work.

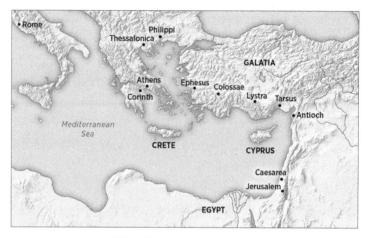

MAP OF THE NEW TESTAMENT WORLD.[3]

QUESTIONS FOR DISCUSSION/REFLECTION

- Who has been the most important spiritual influence in your life, and how have they influenced you?
- How would you describe your influence on others?
- What would you like to change about your influence?
- What are you hoping to get out of this book?
- Why do you think it is important for all Christians to view themselves as influencers?

CHAPTER ONE

The Quest
for Common Ground

Gaining a Hearing with Your Audience

Most of us have experienced common ground with someone and felt how it brings down walls. For example, I'm a musician, and whenever I find out that someone I'm talking to plays an instrument or is a fan of a band I like, I feel an instant kinship with them. I understand them in a way that I didn't before, and I generally like them.

Common ground is found in mundane places: people who grew up in the same area we did, or who went to the same school; people who live in our neighborhoods, like the same food we do, or root for the same sports teams. We can know nothing else about a person, but if we have common ground in just one area, we are more open and friendly with them. Common ground counts for a lot.

Paul knew this. Part of his strategy for spreading the

message of Christianity around the Mediterranean was to seek common ground with anyone who would listen. Plenty of obstacles acted as barriers between people and the gospel of Jesus Christ. Paul and his team needed to find a receptive audience as often as possible. They wanted the message of Christ to fall on friendly ears. As Christian leaders we want the same thing today.

For that to happen, Paul and his team would need to cultivate common ground with their listeners. They accomplished that in many ways, but we're going to focus on two examples: their ministry in synagogues, and Paul's speech in the city of Athens.

COMMON GROUND IN THE SYNAGOGUES

Synagogues were local Jewish community centers that served a variety of purposes, religious and otherwise. Most synagogues had regular services that featured prayer and the reading of the Jewish Scriptures, and some served educational purposes. The temple in Jerusalem was the heart of religious life for all Jews, but thriving Jewish communities could be found in many cities throughout the Roman Empire. For those communities, the synagogue was a place to foster solidarity, friendship, and religious community.

When they came to a new city, Paul and his team typically started in the synagogue (Acts 17:1–2). This was a cornerstone of his team's evangelistic strategy. In fact, the first thing Paul did after becoming a Christian was to preach the gospel in the synagogues of Damascus (Acts 9:20).

Why did Paul start there? Knowing a little bit about Paul's

background gives us the answer. Paul was born into a Jewish family in the city of Tarsus, a cosmopolitan and influential Greco-Roman city on the south coast of modern Turkey (Acts 21:39; 22:3; Phil. 3:5; 2 Cor. 11:22). Tarsus had an intellectual reputation; it was known for its schools and emphasis on learning. It was also an important travel and commercial hub in the region.[1] Like most large cities of the day, Tarsus had a substantial Jewish population. Paul's family and the rest of the Jewish population of Tarsus would have experienced fellowship and camaraderie in the synagogue.

Though Paul was raised in the mainly Greco-Roman environment of Tarsus, he was religiously educated in Jerusalem under the famed rabbi Gamaliel, which meant that he would have spent considerable time in Israel as a young man (Acts 22:3; 26:4).

So Paul had this dual background: he was raised in a city steeped in Greek and Roman culture, but he also had lived within the Jewish community of that city and was educated religiously in Jerusalem. As a result, Paul was able to engage knowledgeably on cultural matters with Greeks, Romans, and Jews. We also know that Paul was multilingual because of this unique background, speaking Greek, Aramaic, and possibly Latin and Hebrew as well (Acts 21:37–40; 26:14).

This diverse language and cultural pedigree enabled Paul to seek common ground with many types of people, especially those with Jewish cultural and religious heritage. When Paul spoke of Jesus as the long-promised Jewish Messiah, synagogue audiences would have been familiar with the Scriptures he used to make his argument—even if they were not ultimately persuaded. Paul could find instant common ground in almost any synagogue, so he always started there if he could.

In many cases, the common ground between Paul and the Jews in these synagogues created enough rapport that they listened and became Christians. In some cases, however, they were hostile to his message (see Acts 13:50; 14:5; 17:5; 18:6; 19:9). The lesson here is that common ground will not *guarantee* a victory in ministry, but it will certainly set the stage for one. Paul clearly thought that the strategy would be effective in the long run, because he and his team continued to start in synagogues even after some negative experiences.

COMMON GROUND IN ATHENS

On Paul's second missionary journey through the Roman world (Acts 15:36–18:22, ca. AD 49–52), he spent time in Athens, Greece, where he had an incredible opportunity to dialogue with the city's intellectual elite. It's one of the most memorable moments in Paul's missionary career, and a perfect case study on seeking common ground.

Luke describes the scene for us in the book of Acts, telling us that Paul's spirit was "provoked within him as he saw that the city was full of idols" (Acts 17:16). This was not entirely unusual, because most of the Mediterranean world worshiped a collection of gods and goddesses. The Greeks and Romans worshiped gods with names that may be familiar to us: Zeus, Poseidon, Athena, Artemis, and others. The Egyptians also had their own set of gods and goddesses that were worshiped across the Mediterranean world: Isis, Horus, Osiris, etc. Polytheism like this was the religious norm of nearly every culture in the ancient world. The Jews and Christians stood out in stark contrast against this religious backdrop because of their monotheistic beliefs.

As a native of Tarsus, Paul was familiar with the religious environment of the Greco-Roman world. Athens, however, was on a new level. As Paul walked the streets of the intellectual hub of the Empire, he found it unusually saturated with statues of pagan deities. The Acropolis, which towered above the city, was teeming with pagan temples and idols. The Parthenon, the imposing temple on the Acropolis, was the temple of Athena, the city's patron goddess. It loomed over the inhabitants below, silently proclaiming the power of a deity who was nothing more than carved stone. This bothered Paul. *A lot.*

The first thing he did was go into the synagogue (as usual), but he also went into the crowded Athenian marketplace and shared Christ with whoever happened to be there (Acts 17:17). Eventually Paul found himself debating with some Greek thinkers, and through that experience was invited to address an important group in Athens: the Areopagus (Acts 17:18–19).

The Areopagus was an ancient Athenian council that oversaw various religious and civic matters. *Areopagus* is a Greek word that translates "Hill of Ares," or more popularly, "Mars Hill." The council got its name from the small hill that sits nearby the larger Acropolis. This was their traditional meeting place.

The council got wind of Paul's message and how he engaged with the Greek philosophers, and they wanted to hear what he had to say. Luke describes what happened next:

They took him and brought him to the Areopagus, saying, "May we know what this new teaching is that you are presenting? For you bring some strange things to our ears. We wish to know therefore what these things mean." Now all the Athenians and the foreigners who lived there would spend their time in nothing except telling or hearing something new. (Acts 17:19–21)

I have to smile every time I read Luke's comment in verse 21. It appears that he found the intellectual climate of Athens to be a little pretentious.

So Paul finds himself standing before this renowned council in Athens. Can you imagine the pressure? Because of how influential the members of the Areopagus were, Paul was in a position to make an exponential impact if he spoke of Christ in a compelling way. What he chose to say is a master class in finding and leveraging common ground.

Paul begins this way:

"Men of Athens, I perceive that in every way you are very religious. For as I passed along and observed the objects of your worship, I found also an altar with this inscription: 'To the unknown god.' What therefore you worship as unknown, this I proclaim to you." (Acts 17:22–23)

Paul starts by commenting on the religious environment in Athens. He doesn't do it in a condemning way, but just as an observant outsider. He tells them that he notices they are very religious, and that as he looked around he saw something unusual—an altar to an unknown god.

The other altars in Athens would have had the names of the gods and goddesses on them, or a representation of the god that was unmistakable. But just to be sure that they weren't forgetting one of the gods and inadvertently offending him or her, the Athenians apparently created this generic altar to an unknown god.[2] Paul's strategy was essentially to say, "That unknown god you worship? I know who he is." After this brief introduction, Paul gets to the heart of the matter:

> "The God who made the world and everything in it, being Lord of heaven and earth, does not live in temples made by man, nor is he served by human hands, as though he needed anything, since he himself gives to all mankind life and breath and everything. And he made from one man every nation of mankind to live on all the face of the earth, having determined allotted periods and the boundaries of their dwelling place, that they should seek God, and perhaps feel their way toward him and find him. Yet he is actually not far from each one of us, for "'In him we live and move and have our being'; as even some of your own poets have said, "'For we are indeed his offspring.' Being then God's offspring, we ought not to think that the divine being is like gold or silver or stone, an image formed by the art and imagination of man." (Acts 17:24–29)

His first words are pretty remarkable if you know something about the physical terrain of Athens. If Paul were standing on the Areopagus addressing the council, it would be quite a claim to say that God doesn't live in temples. The Parthenon and the other temples on the Acropolis were in view as Paul spoke. He may have even gestured toward the temples as he made his point.

A few years ago I had the chance to visit Athens. Here is a photo of me standing on the Areopagus. The Acropolis with its many temples is in the background.

RYAN ON THE AREOPAGUS.
PHOTO BY ASHLEY LOKKESMOE

Paul was saying to the Athenians that, yes, there is a god. It's right to want to know and serve God, but it's wrong to think that He's something we create or that He lives in houses we build for Him. He is not demonizing the Athenians; he is suggesting that they *misunderstand* who God is. Paul describes God as a creator and sustainer, emphasizing His sovereignty over history. These were not entirely foreign concepts to the

Athenians—so once again, Paul is trying to find whatever common ground he can work with.

Next, Paul does something extraordinary. In verse 28, he quotes two Greek poets to describe God: "'In him we live and move and have our being'; as even some of your own poets have said, 'For we are indeed his offspring.'"[3] Paul goes on to argue that since we are God's offspring, He should look something like us since children resemble their parents. How can we be God's children if we are the ones building His statues out of gold or stone? Paul finishes his famous speech to the Areopagus by indirectly introducing Christ:

> "The times of ignorance God overlooked, but now he commands all people everywhere to repent, because he has fixed a day on which he will judge the world in righteousness by a man whom he has appointed; and of this he has given assurance to all by raising him from the dead." (Acts 17:30–31)

Paul introduces the idea of repentance, a key part of Jesus' message, and then refers to Jesus simply as *a man whom [God] has appointed*. He concludes with one brief comment about the resurrection.

What's most notable about Paul's speech is what he *did not* say. Paul did not quote Scripture. He did not mention Israel. He did not mention Jerusalem or the temple. He did not mention the name of Jesus. He did none of that. That sort of thing would be a perfect strategy for a Jewish audience, who would be familiar with the Old Testament and the idea of a Messiah.

But this was not the synagogue. This was an illustrious

council of Athenian thinkers. They were probably unfamiliar with the Jewish Scriptures. Paul knew this, so he sought common ground somewhere else. He commented on their city's religious climate. He leveraged their altar to an unknown god as a launching point. He spoke about God in somewhat generic terms that would not be too confusing or off-putting. He quoted their own poets to back up his claim that God is not something we create.

Paul wanted to find whatever foothold he could to open up a dialogue with the Athenians. He wanted them to feel like he understood them and could speak their language. I'm betting Paul did not view this speech as all he wanted to say, but his best opening statement in what he hoped would become an ongoing discussion. He could more fully explain the gospel through the lenses of Scripture and Jesus' ministry on another occasion; the goal of this initial encounter was to create some intrigue and gain a receptive audience.

Luke tells us that the reaction in Athens was mixed. Some sneered, others wanted to hear him again, and some believed—including a woman named Damaris and a man named Dionysius who happened to be a member of the Areopagus (Acts 17:32–34).

Why was seeking common ground so important to Paul and his team? Paul actually tells us in his own words in 1 Corinthians 9:19–22:

> . . . I have made myself a servant to all, that I might win more of them. To the Jews I became as a Jew, in order to win Jews. To those under the law I became as one under the law (though not being myself under

the law) that I might win those under the law. To those outside the law I became as one outside the law (not being outside the law of God but under the law of Christ) that I might win those outside the law. To the weak I became weak, that I might win the weak. I have become all things to all people, that by all means I might save some.

The phrase *I have made myself a servant to all* could also be translated *I have enslaved myself to all*.[4] Paul put himself in the lowest position possible; he put everyone else first. He spoke to the Jews on Jewish terms and to the Gentiles (non-Jews) on Gentile terms. He became weak to the weak, and so on. Paul tried to be all things to all people.

Why did he do that? He tells us in verse 22: To save people by all means! To win as many as possible to Christ. In fact, he uses the word *win* five times in that passage, each time referring to someone placing their trust in Christ for their salvation.

Paul's hunt for common ground also seems to have been born out of what he expresses in Colossians 4:5–6. "Walk in wisdom toward outsiders, making the best use of the time. Let your speech always be gracious, seasoned with salt, so that you may know how you ought to answer each person."

Seeking common ground is wise because it's disarming. Common ground helps to start conversations off on the right foot. He also said in this text to make *the best use of the time*—i.e., to make the most of every opportunity. Searching for common ground in these different environments was a wise investment of time and enabled Paul and his team to make the most of the opportunities. As we saw in his speech to the Areopagus, Paul seasoned his conversations with salt, peppering in cultural references and appealing to whatever shared heritage he could find.

Another possible motive for Paul's pursuit of common ground is that he had personally experienced what it was like to have someone seek common ground with him. Barnabas had built a relationship with Paul after he became a Christian, and it wasn't necessarily an easy thing for Barnabas to do. Prior to his encounter with Christ, Paul was a notorious persecutor of Christians. He ruthlessly hunted down Christians, imprisoned them, and sought their death (Acts 8:3; 9:2, 21; 22:4–5; 26:10–11; 1 Cor. 15:9; Gal. 1:13).

But the risen Christ showed up and turned Paul around. As soon as Paul became a Christian, he began to preach in the Jewish synagogues (Acts 9:20; 26:20). Eventually he went to Jerusalem to meet the leadership of the church, the disciple Peter and Jesus' brother James (Acts 9:26–28; Gal. 1:18–19).

Paul had a big problem, though. Lots of Christians didn't trust him. They didn't believe he had actually become a Christian, and they were still afraid of him (Acts 9:21, 26; Gal. 1:22–23). Thankfully, Barnabas knew Paul. They had Christ as their common ground, and that was enough for Barnabas to befriend this former persecutor. Barnabas vouched for Paul and told the other Christian leaders that Paul had been preaching fearlessly in the name of Christ (Acts 9:27).

Barnabas helped the other early Christian leaders see that they had spiritual common ground with Paul. In doing so, Barnabas forged a deep friendship and ministry partnership with Paul that would impact many lives for years to come.

WHAT THIS MEANS FOR US TODAY

What can we learn from this strategy of seeking common ground that was so characteristic of Paul's team? The biggest lesson is that we need to change our mentality toward nonbelievers or outsiders. In our culture we often fall into the trap of an "us versus them" mentality when it comes to spiritual matters. This is most evident in the social media environment, which promotes insensitive declarations and hypersensitive responses. We see people as either allies or enemies and quickly put them into one of those two columns based on superficial observations. If someone winds up in the enemy column, they are usually written off as a person who needs to be proven wrong, an opponent.

Paul and his team would have been baffled by this. Paul looked at people who believed very different things from him and asked himself, *How can I build bridges to these people?* Paul wanted as many people as possible to be saved. He tailored his message to the audience; he didn't insist that they acclimate to his preferred presentation. He knew that common ground was the smartest way to put the gospel in the best light.

When is the last time you read an offensive remark on social media and tried to befriend the person who made it? Most of us would never do that, but that's the kind of thing that would be the modern equivalent of Paul's strategy, the twenty-first-century version of becoming all things to all people to win as many as possible.

But this doesn't just happen individually; it happens on a community level, too. We tend to group up with other people who look like us, talk like us, think like us, and live where we live. We often don't realize that we live pretty close to other communities where people think very differently but need Jesus just as much as we do.

Paul and his team went to synagogues first because of the shared religious and cultural heritage. What groups are like that in your community? Maybe people in your community grew up in church and understand the basics, but they've walked away from the faith because it never seemed real to them. They would share some semblance of a religious heritage with you. It just needs to be revived. Find people like that!

Maybe people who live near you are very involved in the community through the schools or kids' sports leagues, but they don't attend church and don't know Jesus. You would have community-based common ground with them. Help them to understand what God's vision is for the community and the next generation.

Maybe other nonprofits in the area are committed to certain efforts that overlap with the mission of the church: food banks, homeless shelters, mentoring programs, prison ministries, etc. The people who volunteer in these organizations may not know Jesus, but they care deeply about people. Help them understand how much Jesus cares about them and the whole world!

Along with changing our attitude toward outsiders, we also need to adjust our speech toward them. When Paul went to Athens, he engaged the intellectual elites on their terms. He spoke confidently and intelligently and did not assume that they thought the way he did. He tried to win them over with his eloquence. We need to do the same thing. We need to season our speech with salt. We need to speak about Christ in a way that is biblical, intelligent, sensitive, compelling, and attractive. We need to stop viewing spiritual conversations as *arguments* that need to be won. We need to instead view our spiritual speech as a mechanism to get to know *people* who need to be won.

Seeking common ground is a powerful tool in the hands of a Christian willing to wield it. It overcomes countless barriers to the gospel. When someone experiences common ground with you, they are more willing to hear what you have to say. They are more willing to consider your perspective. Simply put, they are more likely to *like* you. Common ground gives you a level of influence that you would not otherwise have, because most people are unwilling to be led by someone they don't know or don't like. We should view ourselves as the seekers and wielders of common ground with any people or communities that our ministries touch.

BRONZE PLAQUE OF PAUL'S AREOPAGUS SPEECH (ACTS 17:22–31).
PHOTO BY RYAN LOKKESMOE.

I believe that the pursuit of common ground is one of the most neglected leadership strategies in the church today, despite its being one of the most obvious tactics of Paul and his team. And it was also one of their most effective practices, as history has proven. Today, if you visit Athens, you'll find a bronze plaque with the text of Paul's speech on the side of the Areopagus. In spite of the hill's ancient association with the prestigious Athenian council, history would primarily remember it as the place where Paul offered his persuasive words to the Athenians.

Also, the street that runs alongside the Acropolis in Athens is named after Dionysius, one of the members of the council who became a Christian after Paul's speech (Acts 17:34).

STREET SIGN IN ATHENS. "ROAD OF DIONYSIUS THE AREOPAGITE."
PHOTO BY RYAN LOKKESMOE

Seeking common ground works.

QUESTIONS FOR DISCUSSION/REFLECTION

- What stood out to you about this chapter?
- What places or institutions in your community might be like the synagogue was to Paul? How might you find common ground with people there in order to share Christ?
- What cultural barriers exist in your community that you could work to overcome?
- How could you talk about Christ with nonbelievers in a way that is similar to how Paul spoke to the Athenians?
- Read 2 Corinthians 5:17–21. How does this text relate to the practice of seeking common ground?
- What did you find most challenging about this chapter?
- What is one thing you can change this week based on what you learned in this chapter?
- Suggested Prayer: Lord, I want to look for common ground with those who are far from You. I admit that I am inclined to see differences between myself and others, rather than similarities. I acknowledge that seeking common ground might make me uncomfortable. I need Your guidance and strength to do this. Allow me to see people the way You see them. Show me how to honor You in the way that I befriend and communicate with others. Help me to grasp all that You have done for me so that I am propelled to share the gospel—even with people who seem distant from You or different from me. Amen.

CHAPTER TWO

Watch the Burden

*Monitoring the Expectations
You Place on Others*

When I was in my early twenties, I worked at a hardware store for several months. This was between college and seminary, and I was working three jobs to save up money for an engagement ring and a trip to Europe. I got the job at the hardware store because I had a friend who worked there, but I knew absolutely nothing about the business. This store specialized in selling fasteners (bolts, screws, nuts, etc.), and it seemed like there were a million types.

There was a fairly intense training before I started the job. I was required to memorize every single type of fastener. I had to acquire a working knowledge of a catalog that was the size of a phone book (no exaggeration). After spending some time with the catalog, I was given a written exam. Having demonstrated that I had a basic grasp of the material, I was trained on how to process customer orders and make deliveries. I had learned an immense volume of information before ever clocking in, and I was ready to start working. Or so I thought.

The first day I showed up to the job I had no idea what to do. I knew about fasteners and I had some basic understanding of customer service, but I didn't know what to *do*. I had been given zero instruction about how to spend my time. What should I do first when I got there? How was I supposed to spend eight hours each day? Was every day the same? My supervisors failed to show me how all the information I had learned related to how I was to spend my time.

Over the next several weeks I had to figure it out on my own by incessantly asking questions of my managers, who routinely responded by insinuating that I hadn't been paying attention during the training. I had been given an overwhelming amount of information up front, and I was expected to start immediately behaving as a seasoned hardware store employee.

We do the same kind of thing in the church. Despite our best intentions, we often overburden new believers with too much theological weight, too many required lifestyle changes (some of them unnecessary), and too many church obligations. It's like we expect at the moment of salvation there is going to be a divine download of spiritual maturity that will instantly change the complexion of someone's life. Of course it's true that there is a significant spiritual transformation that occurs when we place our faith in Christ, but spiritual *growth* is a lifelong process. As influencers, we have to get better at showing people how to grow, and we have to normalize the idea that spiritual growth takes time.

Jesus said that His burden is light, and that the experience of finding Him is supposed to feel like a weight being lifted (Matt. 11:28–30). Many new Christians do not experience it that way. In our churches, we are often too zealous up front with new Christians and what we put on their plates. As a result, faith in Jesus can quickly feel like a heavy burden rather than a relief.

This chapter is not a discipleship prescription. Every church is different, and every relationship is unique. If God entrusts you with the privilege and responsibility of guiding someone in their early steps of faith, you must calibrate your approach based on your particular situation. There is no one-size-fits-all solution. This is true if you're leading a good friend, members of your congregation, or your own children.

Rather, this chapter is a case study of one of the most important events in first-century Christianity, the Jerusalem Council. The council can serve as a counterpoint for our tendency to overload people with unnecessary burdens at the beginning of their faith journeys.

THE JERUSALEM COUNCIL AND OUR EXPECTATIONS FOR OTHERS

In the late 40s AD, Paul and Barnabas traveled to the region of Galatia (in modern Turkey), sharing Christ with that area.[1] Afterwards, they returned to their home base of Antioch in Syria. They celebrated with their brothers and sisters in Christ about everything God had done on their missionary journey (Acts 14:26–27). But things were not so rosy in Antioch, because there were some cultural and theological fault lines in the early church that were about to crack open. As Luke records in Acts 15:1, "Some men came down from Judea and were teaching the brothers, 'Unless you are circumcised according to the custom of Moses, you cannot be saved.'"

The cultural rift appearing in Antioch was between Jewish and Gentile Christians. These two groups had different cultural backgrounds and theological vantage points. Before Christianity began to spread through the Roman world, Gentiles worshiped the pantheon of gods and goddesses, and the Jews worshiped the one God of Israel. Now, within the church, these two groups were forging a new community based on their common faith in Christ. But their cultural and theological backgrounds didn't evaporate overnight.

In the case of Antioch, some Christians from a Jewish background were telling Gentiles that salvation required adherence to the law of Moses, which included requirements like circumcision, avoiding certain foods, observing the Sabbath, and participating in certain Jewish festivals. As you can imagine, new Gentile Christians found these requirements disorienting and burdensome.

This division between Jewish and Gentile Christians was an ongoing concern for Paul's team. Galatians, Paul's most fiery letter, deals bluntly with the issue. In Galatians 2:21, Paul says, "If righteousness were through the law, then Christ died for no purpose." Paul is emphasizing that we are not saved because of our willingness to embrace Jewish religious practices; we are saved because of our faith in Christ, regardless of our background.

The question that caused the controversy was essentially this: *How Jewish does someone have to become in order to be Christian?* Some Jews insisted Gentiles needed to follow the law of Moses, but the message of Paul and the other early Christian leaders (who were themselves Jewish) was that it wasn't necessary to be Jewish to become a Christian. But some leaders in some areas were telling converts that they had to first embrace Judaism. These fledgling believers were being unnecessarily weighed down at the outset of their faith, and it was causing confusion and division within the church.

Paul and his friend Barnabas were very proactive about dealing with this trouble. They spoke up in Antioch against those who were insisting that Jewish customs be observed, and when the conflict persisted, they led a delegation south to Jerusalem to settle the matter with the other leaders of the church. In Acts 15:2, Luke describes the scene. "After Paul and Barnabas had no small dissension and debate with them, Paul and Barnabas and some of the others were appointed to go up to Jerusalem to the apostles and the elders about this question."

Paul and Barnabas were bringing others into this important conversation rather than keeping the controversy limited to their own community. The stakes were too high to handle it on their own. Luke describes what happened after they arrived in Jerusalem:

> When they came to Jerusalem, they were welcomed
> by the church and the apostles and the elders, and
> they declared all that God had done with them.
> But some believers who belonged to the party of
> the Pharisees rose up and said, "It is necessary to
> circumcise them and to order them to keep the law
> of Moses." The apostles and the elders were gathered
> together to consider this matter. (Acts 15:4–6)

What transpired next was an early Christian meeting of the minds—Peter, Jesus' lead disciple, addressed the matter by asking this poignant question: "Now, therefore, why are you putting God to the test by placing a yoke on the neck of the disciples that neither our fathers nor we have been able to bear? But we believe that we will be saved through the grace of the Lord Jesus, just as they will" (Acts 15:10–11). In other words, if generations of Jews were not able to keep the law of Moses, how could they expect new Gentile converts to do so?

Then Paul and Barnabas took their turn and told the group what God had done among the Gentiles of Galatia. After hearing all the testimony, James—the leader of the Jerusalem church and Jesus' half brother—stood up and made the decision about how to handle the situation, saying, "My judgment is that we should not trouble those of the Gentiles who turn to God, but should write to them to abstain from the things polluted by idols, and from sexual immorality, and from what has been strangled, and from blood" (Acts 15:19–20). James made it clear that he didn't want to needlessly burden the new Gentile converts to the faith. In fact, the Greek word used in verse 19 that is translated into English as "trouble" is παρενο χλέω (*parenochleo*), a verb that has the connotation of *adding extra difficulties*.[2] The choice of this word implies that there are enough challenges inherent to embracing a new faith; it was unnecessary to make it *more* difficult.

The specific behaviors that James suggested the Gentile believers avoid were evidently the most problematic for these young congregations. Three of them had to do with avoiding certain types of food. The eating habits of Gentiles tended to aggravate cultural divisions with Jews, who were accustomed to the strict food regulations of the law. James was not saying that the Gentiles had to adhere to the law to be saved; he was saying that they would be *wise* to avoid these behaviors because they are a hindrance to enjoying table fellowship with their Jewish brothers and sisters in Christ.

Luke tells us that the council sent a delegation from Jerusalem back to Antioch in order to convey the results of the meeting to the Christians there. Among the delegates were Paul, Barnabas, and Silas, a man who would become a valued member of Paul's team in the years that followed. More on him later.

When Paul and company arrived in Antioch, they shared this letter with the church there:

> The brothers, both the apostles and the elders, to
> the brothers who are of the Gentiles in Antioch and
> Syria and Cilicia, greetings. Since we have heard that
> some persons have gone out from us and troubled
> you with words, unsettling your minds, although we
> gave them no instructions, it has seemed good to us,
> having come to one accord, to choose men and send
> them to you with our beloved Barnabas and Paul,
> men who have risked their lives for the sake of our
> Lord Jesus Christ. We have therefore sent Judas and
> Silas, who themselves will tell you the same things by
> word of mouth. For it has seemed good to the Holy
> Spirit and to us to lay on you no greater burden than
> these requirements: that you abstain from what has
> been sacrificed to idols, and from blood, and from
> what has been strangled, and from sexual immorality.

If you keep yourselves from these, you will do well.
Farewell. (Acts 15:23–29)

Luke tells us how their news was received:

When they were sent off, they went down to Antioch, and having gathered the congregation together, they delivered the letter. And when they had read it, they rejoiced because of its encouragement. And Judas and Silas, who were themselves prophets, encouraged and strengthened the brothers with many words. (Acts 15:30–32)

The Gentile Christians undoubtedly felt a huge sense of relief that their faith could be defined by their relationship with Christ, rather than their adherence to the Jewish law.

Paul and Barnabas showed real leadership in the way that they handled this situation. They knew that ethnic and cultural divisions in the church were at risk of overshadowing the gospel, which was supposed to be good news for everyone. If these sorts of cultural divisions were allowed to take root, and if the Gentile Christians were feeling unnecessarily burdened in their new faith, the church would be damaged significantly. So they proactively contacted the Jerusalem leadership and set the council in motion.

Paul, James, Peter, and the other first-century leaders didn't want to burden new Christians with unnecessary religious or cultural customs. But they also wanted the new Gentile Christians to experience unhindered community with their Jewish Christian brothers and sisters, so they counseled them to avoid certain behaviors that would offend Jewish sensibilities. They encouraged spiritual freedom coupled with cultural sensitivity, liberty mingled with wisdom. They set a great example for us in tone and practice.

WHAT THIS MEANS FOR US TODAY

We don't live in the first-century world with its deep-seated cultural boundaries between Jews and Gentiles, but our culture has its own barriers and taboos. When we see someone on the other side of one of those, we tend to insist that the other person change to be more like us. As influencers in our ministries, families, and communities, we need to understand that it's easy to overburden new believers. We can do this by unrealistically expecting immediate spiritual maturity, or by insisting that new believers adhere to certain behaviors or cultural customs that are not actually required of Christians (which was the case with the Jerusalem Council).

The ones doing the overburdening are often blind to what they're doing, because their efforts are often born out of the best intentions. But if we allow ourselves to create unnecessary challenges for new Christians and make them feel like they're doing this whole Christianity thing wrong, that's a major failure on our part, and it's out of sync with the spirit of the Jerusalem Council.

Whatever spiritual leadership role we occupy, we need to accept one basic reality: people don't change overnight. Most of the time, new believers do not begin behaving like mature Christians right away. Our children probably won't embrace the Christian faith in the way or in the timeline that we might prefer. Over the course of our lives, we will resemble Christ more and more because the Holy Spirit works on us and changes our hearts. As Paul wrote in Romans 8:29, "Those whom he foreknew he also predestined to be conformed to the image of his Son." It takes time to be conformed to Christ's image—a lifetime, in fact—and we never fully arrive as long as we inhabit these earthly bodies. Paul knew this, which is why he sometimes used the metaphor of a race to describe the Christian life (1 Cor. 9:24–25; 2 Tim. 4:7–8).

If you lead in a church context, ask yourself, *What is essential for people to believe and do in order to play a meaningful part in this community?* Try to make your answer as succinct as possible. Whatever your answer is, don't insist that new believers do any more than that in the early stages. Just encourage them, pray for them, and show them a clear path of growth that they can easily explore. Be aware that negative, neutral, or nonexistent feedback from a spiritual leader or mentor can be crushing for a new Christian, so err on the side of warmth and encouragement in the early stages. Help them experience the freedom of knowing Christ, and cast a vision for the renewable joy that awaits them on the path of spiritual growth.

If someone becomes a Christian in your circle of influence, and you know that they believe in Jesus and are increasingly submitting their life to Him, don't insist on too much else early on. Don't awkwardly confront them about their smoking habit. Don't insinuate that they should stop hanging out with their old friends. Don't point it out every time you see a vestige of their old life. Let them know that you love them, and help them fall more deeply in love with Jesus. The Holy Spirit will do the heavy lifting of life change.

The same goes for us parents. If your kid is still working out their faith, don't be afraid of their tough questions. Don't make them feel like they shouldn't ask them. Don't give them weird looks when they listen to *that* music with *those* friends. Don't make them feel like a failure when they're a semester into their freshman year of college and haven't found a church home yet. Be patient. Watch the burden you're imposing on them, because you may not realize that you're adding extra difficulties that are unnecessary, and in the process undermining the gospel of grace.

At our church, Real Hope, we want our process of discipleship to guide people toward greater spiritual maturity while simultaneously *feeling* like a weight is being lifted. To do that, we place the focus on developing a deep understanding of the gospel, and cultivating a vibrant personal relationship with Christ. To aid that process, we encourage people to get into community with other believers so they're not isolated in their spiritual journey. This often means joining a community group and/or serving on a volunteer team. Beyond that we don't ask for much else from new believers. Of course we have higher standards of spiritual maturity for those who want to teach or serve in key leadership roles, because they are setting an example for others. But if you're not in one of those roles, we try to be diligent about keeping the burden light.

Whether we're dealing with friends, church attenders, or our own kids, we need to get real about the fact that many people will hold on to aspects of their pre-Christian lifestyle for a while. We don't need to be rattled by these remnants. If Christ is in someone's life, we can rest assured that God is working on them through the Holy Spirit.

If the Christian life is something like a marathon, as Paul suggested, we need to show people the path, give them water for the journey, and have checkpoints along the way where we can celebrate their progress, and at times, lovingly correct their course. Too often as parents, pastors, bosses, and friends, we try to pack people's bags completely full at the beginning of the race with everything we think they'll ever need for their lifelong spiritual journey. The outcome of that approach is inevitable: the load is too heavy and people tire or give up completely.

Most of this chapter has been concerned with overburdening new believers, because that was the group at the focus of the Jerusalem Council. This tendency to add extra difficulties, however, is a constant risk for seasoned Christians as well. This can take many forms. For parents, we can fall into the trap of placing too much emphasis on rules at the expense of grace. This can warp our kids' perspective of God and themselves. For pastors, we can put too much emphasis in our sermons on practical application without the necessary theological counterbalance of the gospel that puts our good works into proper perspective. This can leave people feeling like they're failing at doing what the pastor suggests, and therefore failing as a follower of Christ.

As influencers, we must remember that most people will assume they have to earn God's love unless they are consistently and vigorously told otherwise. Even if someone grasps the gospel at one time in their life, they can slowly drift back to thinking God won't love them unless they behave like a respectable moral person. If we fail to continually weave the gospel into our spiritual conversations, if we neglect our responsibility to speak of God's grace, we will find ourselves weighed down and overburdening those we influence.

Encountering Christ should be an unburdening experience—an alleviation. It should feel like a profound, joyful relief. Throughout our lives of faith, we Christians should have a deep, abiding sense of freedom because of Christ. As Paul said it, "For freedom Christ has set us free; stand firm therefore, and do not submit again to a yoke of slavery" (Gal. 5:1).

QUESTIONS FOR DISCUSSION/REFLECTION

- What stood out to you about this chapter?
- What was your experience as a new believer? In what ways did you feel unnecessarily overburdened?
- Read the full account of the Jerusalem Council (Acts 15:1–32). What strikes you about this event?
- What does the Jerusalem Council mean for us as influencers?
- How would you be able to tell if you were placing too high of expectations on someone who is new to the faith?
- What *is* important to insist on for new believers?
- What did you find most challenging about this chapter?
- What is one thing you can change this week based on what you learned in this chapter?
- Suggested Prayer: Lord Jesus, help me to remember the gospel of grace—that You died for me not because I'm a good moral person but because You love me. In whatever ways I am striving to earn Your love or favor, please help me to stop. If it is Your will that I lead someone else in the

early stages of their faith, help me to lead and love them well. Guide me in knowing when to encourage them and when to rebuke. Help me, Holy Spirit, to trust that You will do the heavy lifting of life change. Show me the ways in which I might be unnecessarily burdening someone who is seeking You. Reveal to me the ways I am unnecessarily weighing myself down. Amen.

CHAPTER THREE

Offstage Leadership

*Unleashing the Influence
of Behind-the-Scenes Leaders*

When most of us think of leadership—especially within the church—we immediately think of the highly visible "onstage" leaders: pastors, conference speakers, church staff members, worship leaders, etc. Sometimes these onstage leaders don't stand on a physical stage, but they have another form of platform like a popular blog or a large following on social media. As Susan Cain so insightfully pointed out in her book *Quiet*, many of us equate charisma, extroversion, and visibility with leadership, but there is much more to leadership than that.[1]

In reality, onstage leaders are a tiny minority—the tip of the leadership iceberg within our Christian communities. The quiet, overwhelming majority of influencers in God's kingdom are offstage leaders.

Historically speaking, offstage leaders were the type of people who carried letters between the churches in the first century. They were the ones who meticulously copied and preserved the Scriptures throughout the centuries. They were the ones who diligently made sure the poor had enough food to eat and the sick were taken care of. Offstage leaders were the ones through the centuries who had spiritual discussions at home and made sure their children learned the truth about God. They were the ones who carried the gospel to foreign—and sometimes hostile—nations, often doing the incredibly tedious work of translating the Scriptures as they brought Christ to people groups who had never heard of Him.

Today, offstage leaders do many of the same things. They make the Sunday service happen each week at church. They have spiritual discussions with their kids on the way to school. They make an impact on their communities by showing kindness to neighbors. They talk to their coworkers about Christ even when it's a little bit uncomfortable. Offstage leaders volunteer at food pantries, pray for the sick, and welcome guests at church. They enable, amplify, and in many ways outshine the ministry of onstage leaders.

All things considered, offstage leaders are the ones who get it done. No stage. No blog. No significant social media following. They faithfully apply their gifts within the corner of the kingdom that God has entrusted to them, often with little or no fanfare. These are the very people who ministry leaders are constantly trying to find and mobilize.

I've found that church leaders often use a curious strategy when attempting to legitimize and activate offstage leaders.

They point to biblical figures like Moses or Jesus' disciples and cast them as unlikely leaders because of their personal shortcomings or lack of formal education. It's sort of a "If they could do it, you can do it" strategy.

I'm not a fan of this approach. The twelve apostles, for example, were not really offstage leaders at all. Jesus hand-picked them and personally groomed them for future onstage leadership, which grew during His ministry and took off as the church expanded throughout the Roman world. Moses certainly had a huge platform as well, with tens of thousands of Israelites following his lead. It's hard for offstage leaders to relate to these larger-than-life figures.

To inspire and mobilize the offstage leaders in our midst, we need to instead highlight the many biblical influencers who truly were offstage leaders. We need to shine a light on the people who were the supporting cast and crew—the men and women who enabled the full impact of the big-name leaders' ministries. The Bible is full of quiet influencers, and their contribution to the kingdom cannot be overstated. But they're easy to miss because they're usually mentioned briefly and in portions of the Bible we often skip over.

For example, in the gospel of Luke, we find these few verses that highlight some important offstage leaders:

> [Jesus] went on through cities and villages, proclaiming and bringing the good news of the kingdom of God. And the twelve were with him, and also some women who had been healed of evil spirits and infirmities: Mary, called Magdalene, from whom

seven demons had gone out, and Joanna, the wife of Chuza, Herod's household manager, and Susanna, and many others, who provided for them out of their means. And when a great crowd was gathering and people from town after town came to him, he said in a parable, "A sower went out to sow his seed . . ." (Luke 8:1–5)

This is the sort of material that we easily pass over when we read the Bible, because we focus on Jesus' parable that He tells in the verses that come next. But these are the places where we see the important work of offstage leaders. Luke drew attention to the fact that Jesus' ministry was bankrolled, in part, by women—a very significant fact in such a patriarchal climate. When is the last time you thought about how Jesus and His disciples financed their ministry? Luke gives us a glimpse of the behind-the-scenes leadership that was taking place. Joanna is an especially notable example, since she apparently ran in governmental circles.[2]

In the rest of this chapter I will highlight a few members of Paul's team who seem to have operated in an offstage capacity. If you're an onstage ministry leader, I hope this will motivate you to find, deploy, and celebrate these vital behind-the-scenes leaders. If you are more of an offstage type, I hope this will encourage you about the extraordinary influence that you can have in God's kingdom. Also, if an onstage leader has asked for your help, I'm hoping this chapter motivates you to say yes. You are more valuable to the church than you could ever know!

LUKE'S OFFSTAGE LEADERSHIP

Luke is my personal favorite offstage influencer from the New Testament era. I'm fascinated by him, which is why I focused on his writings in my seminary and doctoral studies. It is hard to overstate Luke's impact on the Christian faith today. His writings, Luke and Acts, make up around 27 percent of the New Testament, with a higher total word count than all of Paul's letters combined. Luke wrote more of the New Testament than any other single writer.

As stated in the prologue to his gospel, Luke went around meticulously interviewing eyewitnesses to Jesus' ministry as well as verifying sources (Luke 1:1–4). He was like an investigative journalist. He wrote in the most sophisticated language of any New Testament writer, styling himself as an author in the tradition of celebrated Greek historians like Herodotus and Thucydides. The Acts of the Apostles—the sequel to his gospel—covers the key events of the first few decades after Christ's resurrection, providing an invaluable historical framework for understanding the backdrop of the New Testament letters.

Luke's writings are as theologically rich as they are historically reliable. Some of the most distinctive teachings of Jesus are found only in Luke's gospel—for example, the parables of the Good Samaritan and the Prodigal Son (Luke 10:25–37; 15:11–32). Where would our Christian faith be without his twin literary contributions of Luke and Acts? It's hard to imagine. But Luke seems to have been an offstage leader. He is only mentioned by name three times in the New Testament, each time in passing at the end of one of Paul's letters.

In Colossians 4:14, Paul writes, "Luke the beloved physician greets you, as does Demas." This tells us something of Luke's profession, and that he was with Paul when he wrote Colossians. Philemon, a letter written around the same time as Colossians and also sent to Colossae, also mentions Luke: "Epaphras, my fellow prisoner in Christ Jesus, sends greetings to you, and so do Mark, Aristarchus, Demas, and Luke, my fellow workers" (Philem. 23–24). In what many scholars believe was Paul's final letter before his martyrdom, he once again mentions Luke at the end of 2 Timothy: "Luke alone is with me . . ." (2 Tim. 4:11). Luke may have been one of the last people to see Paul alive.

Beyond these explicit mentions of Luke in the Pauline letters, Luke seems to have subtly highlighted himself in several places—the so-called "We" sections of Acts (16:8–17; 20:5–15; 21:1–18; 27:1–28:16). In the book of Acts, Luke generally chronicled early Christian history as a third-person narrator. On a few occasions, however, he switched to the first-person plural voice. For example, in Acts 16:10, Luke wrote, "When Paul had seen the vision, immediately **we** sought to go on into Macedonia, concluding that God had called **us** to preach the gospel to them." These sections of Acts are believed by many scholars to be portions of Paul's journeys when Luke was physically present. He was noting in these instances that he himself was involved in the narrative.

Let's summarize Luke's contributions: He went around and interviewed eyewitnesses to Jesus' ministry to write a historically and theologically reliable gospel. He traveled with Paul for significant portions of his missionary journeys, and stayed at his side during his imprisonment. Then he wrote the Acts of the Apostles, a companion to his gospel and the earliest historical record we have of the growth of the early church in the first century.[3]

Luke is barely mentioned by name in the Bible, but his writings have echoed down through the centuries to all of us. He is a fantastic example of the kind of influence behind-the-scenes leaders can have.

TYCHICUS'S OFFSTAGE LEADERSHIP

Tychicus is one of those names you might recognize if you've read the New Testament closely, but most of us know little about him. As was the case with Luke, Tychicus was only mentioned a few times, so unless we are proactive in examining those instances, we won't learn much about him. But there's enough material for a compelling picture to emerge.

What we know about Tychicus comes mainly from his travel itineraries, and the brief comments Paul makes about his character. In Acts, Luke tells us that Tychicus accompanied Paul on a portion of his journeys. In Acts 20:4, Luke lists some of Paul's travel companions as he made his way through Greece and Macedonia: "Sopater the Berean, son of Pyrrhus, accompanied him; and of the Thessalonians, Aristarchus and Secundus; and Gaius of Derbe, and Timothy; and the Asians, Tychicus and Trophimus." We know, therefore, that Tychicus was from Asia, which was the name of a Roman province in the western portion of modern Turkey.

That being the case, it is no surprise that Paul dispatched Tychicus with several very important letters meant for that area. At the end of Ephesians, Paul writes, "So that you also may know how I am and what I am doing, Tychicus the beloved brother and faithful minister in the Lord will tell you everything. I have sent him to you for this very purpose, that you may know how we are, and that he may encourage your hearts" (Eph. 6:21–22).

Tychicus was from the province of Asia, and Ephesus was the chief city of that area. So Paul was sending Tychicus back home to his old stomping grounds to carry the letter we call Ephesians to the church in the city of Ephesus. What an important task! Paul describes him as a "beloved brother and faithful minister," speaking to the important role he played on Paul's team and why he was trustworthy to personally carry Paul's letter.

Paul makes similar comments about Tychicus at the end of his letter to the Colossians.

> Tychicus will tell you all about my activities. He is a beloved brother and faithful minister and fellow servant in the Lord. I have sent him to you for this very purpose, that you may know how we are and that he may encourage your hearts, and with him Onesimus, our faithful and beloved brother, who is one of you. They will tell you of everything that has taken place here. (Col. 4:7–9)

Colossae was a small town in the same region as Ephesus, and Paul wanted Tychicus to go there along with Onesimus to deliver the letter we call Colossians as well as a general update on Paul's situation as a prisoner in Rome. It is probable that Tychicus also carried Paul's letter to Philemon, since it concerned Onesimus's return to Colossae (more on that in chapter 7).

Paul mentions Tychicus a couple of other times. At the end of his letter to Titus, Paul writes, "When I send Artemas or Tychicus to you, do your best to come to me at Nicopolis, for I have decided to spend the winter there" (Titus 3:12). Similarly, at the end of 2 Timothy, Paul writes, "Tychicus I have sent to Ephesus" (2 Tim. 4:12).

The picture emerging of Tychicus is that he was a trusted friend and associate of Paul's, and a courier of several important letters that ended up in our New Testament. Can you imagine our New Testament without Ephesians, Colossians, or Philemon? Can you imagine how different the spiritual trajectory of Ephesus and Colossae would have been without Paul's words in those letters? Paul was dependent on people like Tychicus to help him shepherd the many scattered Christian communities around the Mediterranean world. Traveling as much as Tychicus did was an expensive, dangerous, arduous task. We owe him a great debt.

EPAPHRAS'S OFFSTAGE LEADERSHIP

Like Tychicus, Epaphras is one of those names that we easily skip over (or clumsily pronounce) when we read the New Testament. But he played a very important role as the original evangelist of the Lycus Valley, where Colossae, Laodicea, and Hierapolis were located. Paul was not the first one to bring the good news about Jesus to that area—Epaphras was. As Paul wrote in Colossians 1:7–8, "... You learned [the gospel] from Epaphras our beloved fellow servant. He is a faithful minister of Christ on your behalf and has made known to us your love in the Spirit." Epaphras laid the foundation of ministry in Colossae, on which Paul continued to build. Paul mentioned Epaphras again later in the same letter: "Epaphras, who is one of you, a servant of Christ Jesus, greets you, always struggling on your behalf in his prayers, that you may stand mature and fully assured in all the will of God. For I bear him witness that he has worked hard for you and for those in Laodicea and in Hierapolis" (Col. 4:12–13).

Paul used several key phrases to describe Epaphras in his letters, like "fellow servant," "faithful minister," and "servant of Christ Jesus." He also describes him as a prayer warrior on behalf of the Colossians, working hard and traveling far to foster their faith and spiritual growth (Col. 4:12). In his letter to Philemon, Paul says, "Epaphras, my fellow prisoner in Christ Jesus, sends greetings to you" (Philem. 23). This letter gives us another designation for Epaphrus: "fellow prisoner." Take them all together, and you can see that Epaphras was wholeheartedly dedicated to serving the church.

Epaphras first brought the gospel to the Lycus Valley, and then worked tirelessly alongside Paul to help those Christian communities grow in their faith. He prayed, he worked, he ministered, he traveled, and he was eventually imprisoned. If Paul were here today, he would tell us that Epaphras was an invaluable part of his team.

WHAT THIS MEANS FOR US TODAY

Paul knew there was no way he could effectively lead so many far-flung congregations without people like Luke, Tychicus, and Epaphras on his team. There was too much work to be done for Paul to do everything himself. The early church was a loose network of new congregations populated by Christians who were young in their faith. Paul simply did not have the luxury of leading without a team of people working behind the scenes, especially once he was imprisoned.

As a former Pharisee, Paul would have known the Jewish Scriptures well, and would have remembered how Moses delegated to other leaders in order to lead effectively during their time in the desert. Moses's father-in-law Jethro had famously given him a healthy perspective on leadership: "You and the people with you will certainly wear yourselves out, for the thing is too heavy for you. You are not able to do it alone" (Ex. 18:18).

Paul could not bear the heavy load of leading all of these churches by himself, particularly in a climate of escalating persecution and when travel was so slow and dangerous. Paul needed offstage leaders who kept the machinery of ministry running.

Luke did his research and created a master two-volume work that would have an exponential impact in the centuries to come. Epaphras and Tychicus spent a lot of time alone, on the road, facing constant danger in order to carry their precious cargo: the gospel of Jesus Christ and letters from Paul to young churches that desperately needed guidance.

What does this mean for us today? It means that if God has entrusted us with an onstage leadership role in His church, we must understand that we were never meant to lead alone. God has surrounded us with gifted offstage leaders who can and will make significant contributions to the ministry, perhaps more significant than our own. Paul didn't lead alone. Why should we?

Paul allowed people to see that he was vulnerable—that he *needed* them. We must be willing to show the same transparency about our limits. We need to look around us for the fellow workers that God has put in our circle, people who can work behind the scenes to do great things for the kingdom. If you're an onstage leader, find these people and let them take stuff off your plate! They'll probably do it better than you if you'll let them. Let those offstage leaders set an agenda based on their gifts that you might not have even considered. Give them some control. Trust them. Maintain relationships with them, as Paul did.

Then follow Paul's example from his letters and shine a light on them. Give them credit! View them as equals and find ways to acknowledge them as partners. When Paul described people like Luke, Epaphras, and Tychicus he often used words with the Greek prefix *syn-*, which we often translate as "fellow." The *syn-* prefix conveyed the idea of doing something *with* someone else. It was a marker of equality.

For example, Paul calls Luke and others his συνεργός (*synergos*), which we translate as "fellow worker." That's where our English word *synergy* comes from. It means to work together. Epaphras and Tychicus are described by Paul with the word σύνδουλος (*syndoulos*), or "fellow servant." Paul viewed them as his partners in ministry, and his language clearly reflected that.

If, on the other hand, you are more of an offstage leader, you need to understand that God might want to use you in a significant way, as a fellow worker with those onstage leaders you see around you. My encouragement to you is this: get in the game. Onstage leaders need you, whether they readily admit it or not. You might be one of those people like Luke, or Epaphras, or Tychicus, or the women who provided financially for Jesus' ministry.

For example, in terms of numbers and degree of influence, parents are the most influential bunch of leaders in the church—and most of them are offstage leaders. They have the opportunity to invest in the next generation on a minute-by-minute basis (literally). Grandparents are another powerful influence within the church as they share their wisdom and experiences with their grandchildren. Other family members can play similar roles. We may not think of our parents or grandparents as church leaders since most of them don't hold formal leadership titles, but their behind-the-scenes influence can impact the spiritual landscape of entire family trees.

Just because you don't have a stage, a microphone, or a popular blog does not mean that God doesn't have an important role for you to play. You can influence from an offstage position in ways that will change lives. I wonder if Luke ever imagined his writings would endure for so long. It's probable that Epaphras and Tychicus did not realize the letters they carried would continue to influence our spiritual lives in the twenty-first century. Don't sell yourself short. God has a beautiful purpose for your influence if you'll make it available to Him.

QUESTIONS FOR DISCUSSION/REFLECTION

- What stood out to you about this chapter?
- Why do you think that leadership is often equated with visibility or extroversion?
- What are some unique ways that offstage influencers can provide leadership for the church today?
- Can you think of any other offstage leaders in Scripture that made a big impact?
- Who has been the most influential offstage leader in your spiritual life? How did God use them to help you grow?
- What did you find most challenging about this chapter?
- What is one thing you can change this week based on what you learned in this chapter?
- Sample Prayer: Lord, help me to see my influence the way You see it. Help me not to have too high an opinion of it, and help me not to sell it short. I want to steward my influence as a gift from You, so show me how to use it. Lead me out of my comfort zone to fulfill the purpose You have for me. I trust You, and I submit to Your leading. Amen.

CHAPTER FOUR

More Than a Ceasefire

Reviving Relationships after Disagreements

I t seems inevitable that famous leaders turn to marble—or perhaps stained glass—over the years. Through the telescope of history, we no longer see them as human beings with complex emotional landscapes; we view them as heroes or saints, as unchanging embodiments of their most famous achievements. Think of the marble monuments in Washington, D.C., the stained-glass windows of a great cathedral, or the oil paintings in renowned museums. Those people represented don't seem real to us. They've been immortalized and sanitized. As a result, we don't relate to them. They seem to be another species of leader altogether.

The complex relationship between Thomas Jefferson and John Adams is a perfect illustration of how unrealistic our perceptions are of famous historical figures. Jefferson has a memorial in D.C., and he is on the $2 bill (if you can find one). He was from the powerful colony of Virginia, and is best known for being the third US president and brilliant wordsmith behind the Declaration of Independence. Thousands of visitors tour his stately home Monticello every year, and generations of students have graduated from the University of Virginia, which he founded.

John Adams was a Massachusetts man. A lawyer, Adams was one of the great minds of the Revolutionary generation. At the first Continental Congress, he argued passionately and persuasively for independence. It is hard to overstate his influence in the Revolutionary era. It was John Adams who nominated George Washington to lead the Continental army. He also chose Thomas Jefferson to draft the Declaration of Independence. Adams went on to serve as George Washington's vice president, and then to lead the nation as America's second president.

Early in the Revolutionary era, Adams and Jefferson had been allies. They came from different colonies and held very different views on the role of government, but they knew each other personally and respected each other. They were friends. Their families spent time together. Adams and Jefferson struggled together to forge a new nation in the face of long odds and a highly uncertain future. In the words of Pulitzer Prize–winning historian Joseph Ellis, Jefferson and Adams were "charter members of the band of brothers who had shared the agonies and ecstasies of 1776 as colleagues. No subsequent disagreement could shake this elemental affinity."[1]

But they did have a disagreement that rattled their friendship to the core. When Thomas Jefferson was serving as vice president, he secretly hired a shady reporter to publish negative stories about John Adams—his friend—who also happened to be the president at the time. When Jefferson defeated Adams in the 1800 election, these two old friends did not speak for twelve years.

Ultimately it was Benjamin Rush, a fellow Founding Father, who facilitated their reconciliation. He encouraged Adams to write to Jefferson and resume their friendship, famously writing to Adams, "I consider you and him, as the North and South poles of the American Revolution.—Some talked, some wrote—and some fought to promote & establish it, but you, and Mr. Jefferson *thought* for us all."[2]

From his home in Massachusetts, called Peacefield, John Adams wrote to Jefferson, who replied from his Virginia plantation, Monticello. What followed was fourteen years of letters between the two men, incrementally reviving their friendship and together reflecting on the serious era of history through which they had both lived and led. As Ellis so eloquently put it, "The friendship, so long in storage, had never completely died."[3]

In one of the most remarkable coincidences of history, these two friends, John and Thomas, died on the same day, July 4, 1826, which also happened to be the fiftieth anniversary of the Declaration of Independence.

Knowing this story pulverizes the marble versions of Thomas Jefferson and John Adams. They are no longer silent, immortal heroes, but complex emotional men who struggled greatly in their lives. They had the ability to hurt each other and to be hurt. Jefferson's pride led him to publicly humiliate his friend, and Adams's pride led him to quietly obsess for years about how to vindicate himself and expose Jefferson. This story makes the two men human to us.

The most notable thing about this story is how *unusual* it is. It is rare for personal relationships to be broken in such a significant way and then later be restored. I don't mean simply returning to speaking terms or eking out a begrudging apology. I mean a genuine restoration of friendship, in which the former division begins to seem absurd and fades from memory.

In the same way that Jefferson and Adams's contentious relationship muddies our glossy view of them, there is a story about Paul that may shatter our stained-glass view of him.

A FAMILY FEUD

This episode involves our old friends Paul and Barnabas. The Jerusalem Council decision had just come down, and they were about to leave Antioch and head west to continue spreading the gospel. They were filled with optimism, ready to go out into the world and tell people about the freedom and hope that they could find in Christ. But there was a speed bump ahead of them, and it involved a man named Mark. Let's rewind a little bit and discover how Mark originally became a part of Paul's team.

In the book of Acts, Luke tells us that there was a famine in Judea and the church there was struggling. The relatively wealthy church to the north in Antioch decided to send aid to the Judean Christians, and that relief was carried to Jerusalem by Paul and Barnabas (Acts 11:27–30).

Around that same time, Peter was arrested and imprisoned

because of his public ministry in Jerusalem. Luke recounts how Peter was miraculously freed from prison, going immediately "to the house of Mary, the mother of John whose other name was Mark, where many were gathered together and were praying" (Acts 12:12).

Mark was apparently a nickname, and his family ran in the same circles as the disciples and the rest of the Jerusalem Christian community. We also find out later in one of Paul's letters that Mark was Barnabas's cousin (Col. 4:10). Luke tells us that after their time in Jerusalem, "Barnabas and Saul returned from Jerusalem when they had completed their service, bringing with them John, whose other name was Mark" (Acts 12:25).

Soon afterwards, the church at Antioch commissioned Paul and Barnabas for their first missionary journey. Luke describes their departure: "Being sent out by the Holy Spirit, they went down to Seleucia, and from there they sailed to Cyprus. When they arrived at Salamis, they proclaimed the word of God in the synagogues of the Jews. And they had John to assist them" (Acts 13:4–5). Mark came along with them on the journey that started out on the island of Cyprus, though Luke refers to him by his other name, John.

After the trio made their way through Cyprus, the time came to head north across the water to the southern coast of Turkey—and this is where it gets interesting. Luke writes, "Now Paul and his companions set sail from Paphos and came to Perga in Pamphylia. And John left them and returned to Jerusalem" (Acts 13:13). Without elaboration, Luke mentioned John's (Mark's) departure before continuing to narrate Paul and Barnabas's journey. That's not the whole story.

Later, after Paul and Barnabas returned to their home base of Antioch, they became mired in the controversy that led to the Jerusalem Council. Afterwards, when they decided to head out from Antioch on another missionary journey, Luke describes what happened:

> After some days Paul said to Barnabas, "Let us return and visit the brothers in every city where we proclaimed the word of the Lord, and see how they are." Now Barnabas wanted to take with them John called Mark. But Paul thought best not to take with them one who had withdrawn from them in Pamphylia and had not gone with them to the work. And there arose a sharp disagreement, so that they separated from each other. Barnabas took Mark with him and sailed away to Cyprus, but Paul chose Silas and departed, having been commended by the brothers to the grace of the Lord. And he went through Syria and Cilicia, strengthening the churches. (Acts 15:36–41)

The Greek word in verse 39 that is translated as "sharp disagreement" is παροξυσμός (*paroxysmos*), which means a "severe argument based on intense difference of opinion."[4] The word implies a bitter, acrimonious argument.[5] Put more plainly, Paul and Barnabas had it out over this Mark situation. They disagreed so bitterly that Paul couldn't even imagine working with Barnabas or Mark. They went their separate ways. Paul continued on with his new friend Silas, who had come to Antioch after the Jerusalem Council, leaving Mark and Barnabas to go their own way. Paul had just helped to broker the unifying outcome of the Jerusalem Council, and now he couldn't find a way to work through his differences with Barnabas and Mark. He had to physically separate from them in order to continue in ministry.

We don't know exactly what the next decade of Paul's relationship with Mark and Barnabas looked like, but we know that reconciliation happened to some extent. In the early 60s AD (over a decade later), Mark shows up in a few of Paul's letters, and it's clear they're working together in ministry again. There's no detailed description of Mark's role; he's just mentioned in passing. If you're reading Paul's letters and you're not clued in to the backstory, you might not even notice Mark's name or connect it to the falling out that happened in Acts 15.

As far as Paul's relationship with Barnabas specifically, we're not sure how it turned out. Paul does mention Barnabas a few times in his letters, but we have no direct indication that they worked together again.[6] This does not mean that they didn't reconcile; it's very possible they did. We just don't have the explicit evidence for it as we do with Mark. Let's see how God revived Paul and Mark's relationship.

Paul was sitting in a Roman prison awaiting trial before Caesar, and he was writing letters to encourage churches. Toward the end of one of these letters, Colossians, Paul mentions Mark:

> Aristarchus my fellow prisoner greets you, and Mark the cousin of Barnabas (concerning whom you have received instructions—if he comes to you, welcome him), and Jesus who is called Justus. These are the

only men of the circumcision among my fellow
workers for the kingdom of God, and they have been
a comfort to me. (Col. 4:10–11)

That's all Paul says about Mark in this letter, but it tells us a few things.

First, we know that Mark is with Paul in Rome (or in its vicinity), because Paul says hello to the Colossian Christians from Mark. Second, we learn that Mark is actively engaged in ministry, because Paul called him "a fellow worker for the kingdom of God," and apparently the Colossians have already received instructions from Paul to welcome Mark if he visits. Third, Paul includes Mark in the group of people who have been a comfort to him during his imprisonment. That's a far cry from Acts, when Paul didn't even want to travel with Mark! Paul also mentions Mark at the end of his letter to Philemon, a brief letter written around the same time and also sent to the church in Colossae (Philem. 24).

The most telling reference to Mark is found at the end of 2 Timothy—widely believed to be Paul's final letter before his martyrdom. Paul is in prison again, and in his final words to Timothy he wrote, "Luke alone is with me. Get Mark and bring him with you, for he is very useful to me for ministry" (2 Tim. 4:11). At one time Mark was useless to Paul—so useless that he parted ways with Barnabas over the matter. Now he was *very useful* to Paul for his ministry.

Mark had also become indispensable to Peter, who was engaged in ministry in Rome around the same time. In the final verses of 1 Peter, the apostle sends his greetings and says, "So does Mark, my son" (1 Peter 5:13). The Mark that

Peter mentioned is widely believed to be the same Mark who was in Paul's circle.

According to early Christian historical sources, Mark served as Peter's interpreter in Rome during the final years of the apostle's life. After Peter's death, Mark—the man who at one time Paul thought unworthy as a travel companion— went on to write the gospel of Mark, based in large part on Peter's testimony.[7]

WHAT THIS MEANS FOR US TODAY

Despite Mark's painful split with Paul, God had big plans for him. We don't know exactly how their reconciliation came about, but their resumed ministry partnership is a poignant example for us. It doesn't mean their reunion was easy. Luke says that Paul had a very bitter disagreement with Barnabas over Mark, and Paul probably didn't see them again for a long time afterward, judging by the painfully slow rate of communication at that time and the uncertain itineraries of these early evangelists. Paul, Barnabas, and Mark must have been proactive about working through their issues when they had the opportunity to do so.

Jesus said, "Blessed are the peacemakers, for they shall be called sons of God" (Matt. 5:9). This means that if you seek peace, you are exhibiting one of God's family traits. Jesus, in fact, was the ultimate peacemaker. Paul knew this, and wrote about it in his letter to the Colossians: "In [Christ] all the fullness of God was pleased to dwell, and through him to reconcile to himself all things, whether on earth or in heaven, making peace by the blood of his cross" (Col. 1:19–20).

The problem is that making peace is extremely difficult, even for the most humble among us. It's counterintuitive and countercultural. Peacemaking flies in the face of our individualistic society that prizes self-expression and its evil twin, self-vindication. Peacemaking requires us to acknowledge our pride and willfully set it aside.

Our culture has a personality, too, and peacemaking is out of sync with that personality. People who hold grudges, who speak their mind with no reservations, who appear uncompromising, are often admired. These, however, are not the attributes of a peacemaker. These are not the qualities of a godly influencer.

Jesus' message about making peace was countercultural in the first century, and it's countercultural now. It has never been easy to make peace, and it never will be. That's why it takes real leadership to view yourself as peacemaker and to act accordingly. The sad truth is that more often than not, if *you* do not take the responsibility to act as a peacemaker, no one will.

Families need peacemakers. Workplaces need peacemakers. Governments need peacemakers. Communities need peacemakers. Peace does not happen automatically. True peace—not just a ceasefire—is hard-fought and must be humbly maintained through prayer and proactive measures. Peace does not happen through passive aggression or ignoring conflict.

Peacemakers are a rare breed, and we desperately need more of them in the church. Today we experience all sorts of divisions in church leadership, and there is no shortage of opportunities for a lack of peace. Ministry is a high-stakes environment with deep emotional investment. Even relatively minor differences in ministry philosophy can cause major hurts and division, and it's very easy for ministry discord to become personal. I've experienced this and it really does hurt. Once that wound is there, it's very hard to find peace and unity without deliberate and sustained effort. And it often doesn't feel like any sort of victory while you're in the middle of the process.

This is why Jesus' disciple Peter encouraged us to "seek peace and pursue it" (1 Peter 3:11). The language Peter used has the connotation of persistent striving for peace. He knew that peace wasn't easy. He heard Jesus say the words, "Blessed are the peacemakers," and he experienced what a high calling it is.

Perhaps the simplest place to start is to acknowledge that conflicts will happen. There's no way to avoid them, because we are humans and we sin. The key is how we respond afterwards when we're angry or hurt, when we're not at our best and not seeing ourselves very clearly.

The lesson from Paul and his team is this: don't write people off. It's the easiest thing to do, but God might have great plans in the future for you and that person if you're willing to fight for it. He might want to revive your relationship for His purposes! God might have a Jefferson/Adams or Paul/Mark story in mind for you. If we can remove our bruised egos from the equation and choose to follow in the footsteps of Paul, we can model a countercultural grace to a world that is watching. God specializes in reconciliation, and it's wonderful when it happens.

QUESTIONS FOR DISCUSSION/REFLECTION

- What stood out to you about this chapter?
- Have you ever had a falling out/reconciliation with someone? What did God teach you through that experience?
- Why is peacemaking so difficult?
- In what ways are Christians uniquely equipped to be peacemakers in our circles of influence? What's at stake if Christian influencers don't view themselves as peacemakers? What do we lose?
- How might God use peacemaking to bring people into a relationship with Him?
- What did you find most challenging about this chapter?
- What is one thing you can change this week based on what you learned in this chapter?
- Sample Prayer: Heavenly Father, I want to be a peacemaker. I want to exhibit that family trait. I realize that my pride gets in the way of acknowledging reconciliation that needs to occur, and it interferes in my willingness to seek peace. Please humble me in this area. Show me if there is anyone in my life with whom I need to seek peace. If someone attempts to seek peace with me, help me to respond with grace, not cynicism. Please guide me, Holy Spirit. I trust You. Amen.

CHAPTER FIVE

Worthy Conflicts

Contending for What Actually Matters

The life of a Christian influencer is a minefield of potential conflict. Any experienced pastor will tell you that, but this reality is not unique to pastoral ministry. The same challenge lies before anyone trying to be a godly influence on anyone else. We find ourselves having to cope with a constant stream of slights, misrepresentations, criticisms, and comparisons. These experiences are like waves crashing on a beach. They just keep coming.

In some instances these waves of negativity are unfair or unfounded personal criticism. Some of them are less personal, like questions of theology or ministry practice. Regardless, those of us who serve in ministry leadership positions have the unrelenting task of searching our hearts in real time and determining if something is worth engaging. Is it something worth pushing back on, or are our egos just bruised? It's hard to tell when so often we're tired and emotionally spent.

The world of politics is similarly hazardous. Abraham Lincoln, the greatest leader I'm aware of in any modern context, had a very interesting coping mechanism for the onslaught of criticisms that came his way. Lincoln would write blunt, scathing letters to his opponents—and then not send them. In his classic book, *Lincoln on Leadership*, Donald T. Phillips describes Lincoln's distinctive practice:

> One of Lincoln's most effective methods of dealing with harsh criticism was to write extended letters of refutation. Often, in order to vent his anger and frustration, he would sit down at his desk, compose a letter of denial, and then walk away without sending it. He felt better for having stated his case but did not want any of his angry or emotional remarks made public.[1]

After learning that Lincoln did this, I've gotten in the habit of rehearsing what I would say to someone who I feel has wronged me. It might seem strange, but it's been healthy and helpful for me. I find that one of two things usually happens: As I hear my thoughts become audible, I can hear how prideful or insecure they are in a way I couldn't when they were silent thoughts inside my head. Usually this leads me to just drop it and move on. Or, I feel that my anger or hurt feelings are legitimate, and I experience some level of relief at having said it aloud, if only to myself. It's cathartic, and it's usually enough to help me move on, even if I think I have been genuinely wronged.

Sometimes there's a third outcome of these imagined dialogues: I realize that the matter needs to be addressed. A confrontation needs to happen. If this is the case, I've had at least one dry run of articulating how I'm feeling. That way, when the necessary conversation happens, I'm not clumsily improvising on the fly. I've rehearsed it at least once and have some sense of what to say and what *not* to say.

No matter what sort of influence we have, we all need to understand what it looks like to choose our battles and handle criticism in a Christlike manner. Parents need to learn this, as do employees and employers. Teachers, politicians, coaches, friends, siblings, sons, daughters, neighbors—we all need to learn which sorts of conflict are worth our time and emotional energy. Lincoln set an example for us, and now we will see how Paul and his team handled similar circumstances.

PAUL IN CONFLICT

What was Paul's view of conflict? How did he handle the struggle of personal criticism, and how did he advise his teammates on how to navigate the minefield of potential conflict? What was worth fighting over? As we'll see, Paul was sooner to avoid conflict than to engage in it.

Avoiding Conflict

The church in Corinth was riddled with conflict, and some of their angst was directed personally toward Paul. His response sets a great example for us. In 1 Corinthians, Paul is responding to divisions in the church regarding which leaders to follow. Paul had no time for this sort of meaningless division, writing these words on the subject:

> I appeal to you, brothers, by the name of our Lord Jesus Christ, that all of you agree, and that there be no divisions among you, but that you be united in the same mind and the same judgment. For it has been reported to me by Chloe's people that there is quarreling among you, my brothers. What I mean is that each one of you says, "I follow Paul," or "I follow Apollos," or "I follow Cephas," or "I follow Christ." Is Christ divided? Was Paul crucified for you? Or were you baptized in the name of Paul? (1 Cor. 1:10–13)

Paul was addressing the fact that some people in the Corinthian congregation were more enamored with the leadership of Jesus' disciple Peter (referred to here by his Aramaic nickname, Cephas), or that of another early Christian leader, Apollos. Luke had this to say about Apollos in the book of Acts:

> A Jew named Apollos, a native of Alexandria, came to Ephesus. He was an eloquent man, competent in the Scriptures. He had been instructed in the way of the Lord. And being fervent in spirit, he spoke and taught accurately the things concerning Jesus. . . . And when he wished to cross to Achaia, the brothers encouraged him and wrote to the disciples to welcome him. When he arrived, he greatly helped those who through grace had believed, for he powerfully

refuted the Jews in public, showing by the Scriptures that the Christ was Jesus. (Acts 18:24–28)

Apollos was an effective teacher who taught about Jesus in powerful and persuasive ways. He was gifted. Peter had been Jesus' lead disciple, so it makes sense that some people would be drawn to him. Paul could have easily been threatened by these other two leaders: a gifted teacher and a close associate of Jesus. But his main concern was not defending himself; it was preserving unity.

After continuing his discussion on the matter, he comes to this distinctly Christian statement on leadership: "I planted, Apollos watered, but God gave the growth. So neither he who plants nor he who waters is anything, but only God who gives the growth" (1 Cor. 3:6–7). God is the one who is changing lives, so it's misguided to pledge allegiance to one leader over another and allow those allegiances to cause discord. For Paul, his pride was not worth fighting for—but *unity* was.

There were indeed times when Paul defended his status as an apostle, but when he did he put the focus on God and not his own personal gifts or talents. For example, in 2 Corinthians 11:22–30, Paul boasts about all the trials and struggles he had been through in his effort to share Christ with the world. At the end of that section, Paul closed with the words, "If I must boast, I will boast of the things that show my weakness" (2 Cor. 11:30). Paul was a master at deflecting unnecessary conflict, and he did so by taking the focus off himself as much as possible.

When Paul wrote to two of his coworkers, Timothy and

Titus, he advised them to adopt the same posture of avoiding needless conflict. When writing to Titus, he said, "Avoid foolish controversies, genealogies, dissensions, and quarrels about the law, for they are unprofitable and worthless" (Titus 3:9). He wrote similar words to Timothy: "Have nothing to do with foolish, ignorant controversies; you know that they breed quarrels. And the Lord's servant must not be quarrelsome but kind to everyone, able to teach, patiently enduring evil, correcting his opponents with gentleness" (2 Tim. 2:23–25).

In both passages, Paul described quarreling as foolishness. Christian influencers of any kind, according to Paul, should patiently endure criticism and avoid engaging in conflict when possible. Paul's main concern was the preservation of unity, and worthless arguing was threatening to divide these young communities. We are at risk of the same disunity in our families and congregations if we don't follow Paul's example.

Engaging in Conflict

While Paul cared deeply about avoiding conflict when it came to personal pride and superficial frictions, there was one area where he was uncompromising: the gospel. Paul would not stand for false teaching and perversions of the gospel. In addition to fighting for unity, Paul consistently and *vehemently* defended the true gospel of Jesus Christ against those who would distort it. That was—and still is—a worthy conflict.

Paul's letter to the Galatians is the angriest of his letters, written around the time of the Jerusalem Council. As we discussed in chapter 2, there were people telling Gentile converts to Christianity that they had to observe Jewish religious practices in order to be a real Christian. That sort of false teaching undermined the gospel of grace that was freely available to everyone regardless of their background, and it made Paul furious to find out that people were infiltrating the congregations he founded and introducing this warped version of the gospel. Paul's anger, which he was so skillful at hiding in many incendiary situations, is right at the surface in Galatians. He's not even trying to hide it. After the briefest of pleasantries at the beginning of the letter, Paul writes:

> I am astonished that you are so quickly deserting him who called you in the grace of Christ and are turning to a different gospel—not that there is another one, but there are some who trouble you and want to distort the gospel of Christ. But even if we or an angel from heaven should preach to you a gospel contrary to the one we preached to you, let him be accursed. (Gal. 1:6–8)

There is only one true gospel, and Paul would not stand for its distortion. He had no sympathy for those who peddle counterfeit gospels, and Paul was uncompromising in his battle to restore truth. That is a battle that Paul believed was worth fighting.

A little later in Galatians, Paul describes a time when he dramatically confronted Peter in public because Peter was lending credibility (perhaps unwittingly) to those who were advocating for the necessary practice of Jewish customs. Paul describes this scene in Galatians (referring again to Peter as Cephas):

> When Cephas came to Antioch, I opposed him to
> his face, because he stood condemned. For before
> certain men came from James, he was eating with
> the Gentiles; but when they came he drew back and
> separated himself, fearing the circumcision party.
> And the rest of the Jews acted hypocritically along
> with him, so that even Barnabas was led astray by
> their hypocrisy. But when I saw that their conduct
> was not in step with the truth of the gospel, I said to
> Cephas before them all, "If you, though a Jew, live
> like a Gentile and not like a Jew, how can you force
> the Gentiles to live like Jews?" (Gal. 2:11–14)

When Paul saw behaviors that were contrary to the free-ing truth of the gospel, especially among the leadership, he confronted it unapologetically—even publically ("I said to Cephas *before them all* . . ."). Remember, Paul and Barnabas were a driving force of convening the Jerusalem Council in the first place, which dealt with this same subject.

As we've seen, Paul was willing to fight for two things: the truth of the gospel, and unity among believers. Paul realized that those two issues are often intertwined. In 1 Timothy he wrote about how a lack of understanding of the true gospel leads to disunity:

> If anyone teaches a different doctrine and does not
> agree with the sound words of our Lord Jesus Christ
> and the teaching that accords with godliness, he is
> puffed up with conceit and understands nothing.
> He has an unhealthy craving for controversy and

for quarrels about words, which produce envy, dissension, slander, evil suspicions, and constant friction among people who are depraved in mind and deprived of the truth . . . (1 Tim. 6:3–5)

A distorted gospel feeds an unhealthy craving for quarrels, which lead to continual friction. These subjects—the gospel and unity among believers—were worthwhile conflicts for Paul and his team. These were the fights that really mattered to Paul, and they should matter to us.

WHAT THIS MEANS FOR US TODAY

Paul's policy of standing for the truth while deflecting unnecessary conflicts finds its inspiration in Jesus Himself. Jesus had all sorts of false accusations hurled against Him, especially during His trial before the Jewish leadership and the Roman governor Pontius Pilate. Jesus did not respond to or deny most of the accusations. He was so quiet, in fact, that Pilate was baffled by His refusal to answer His accusers. John records Pilate's response:

> He entered his headquarters again and said to Jesus, "Where are you from?" But Jesus gave him no answer. So Pilate said to him, "You will not speak to me? Do you not know that I have authority to release you and authority to crucify you?" (John 19:9–10)

The mission was more important to Jesus than defending Himself or proving that His accusers were wrong. People mocked Jesus, and He did nothing to stop it. Jesus called us to love our enemies—to *love* them. Not just to tolerate them. If that's the standard—to love those who might *hate* us—how much more should we love people we serve with who might have offended us? How much more should we love our family members and friends who have said misguided things about us?

Paul seems to have adopted this Christlike posture: mockery isn't worth engaging. Insults aren't worth a response. The mission is more important, and unnecessary quarreling derails the mission. The gospel is what matters, and the unity it fosters among brothers and sisters in Christ.

What does all this mean? We're so far removed from the Jew/Gentile controversies of the first century, and sometimes it can feel difficult to relate to the extraordinary circumstances facing Paul and his team. But there are a few root lessons that we can all take to heart.

First, no matter what sort of leadership role we play, we should be very slow to initiate a conflict. We need to decide what is worth defending and find ways to cope with whatever offenses don't rise to that level. We all need to find a mechanism, like Lincoln did, to blow off steam and avoid adding fuel to a fire that actually needs extinguishing.

Second, we need to remember that Satan wants us mired in disagreements. He wants to stir up a multitude of small perceived offenses in our hearts in order to keep us in a perpetual state of anger or bitterness, which cripples our ability to reflect Christ. Satan wants to keep us focused on ourselves, to turn our ministries into mechanisms of propping up our ego. One of his classic tactics is to dress pride up and disguise it from us so that we don't think it's pride.

When we are unjustly criticized about something, we have an instinctive desire to correct the record and defend our reputation. I have personally experienced the frustration of unfounded criticism, and I'm sure I will many times in the future. In one instance, I moved across the country to attend seminary and found out that some of my friends back home were saying unkind (and untrue) things about my motives for pursuing a theological education. That stung. On another occasion, I left a job to discover that a few of my former colleagues were doing something similar—calling into question my reasons for leaving and concocting a revisionist history of my time as their coworker. That really hurt. Then there are situations that pastors routinely deal with, like frustrated church members talking about me to everyone *but* me.

In those painful moments, I've learned to pray and ask God to give me self-control and peace about not defending myself. I realized that even if I responded by simply telling the truth to correct the record, my goal was still, in part, a prideful one. I cared too much about my reputation. It was my pride masquerading as a desire for justice.

We are all influencers, and if we try to defend everything that comes our way we will forfeit that influence. We will be viewed as thin-skinned, combative, or insecure. We will lose our voice. We must get used to the uncomfortable fact that as Christian influencers, we will have many gift-wrapped potential conflicts coming our way in the future. We do not have to unwrap them all. We do not have to unwrap *most* of them. As Donald T. Phillips so eloquently put it:

Every man of courage must, sooner or later, deal with unjust criticism. And all individuals who lead other people . . . likely will be subjected to severe criticism as well as personal attacks on their honor and character. Lincoln realized this fact of life and was prepared for it, as every leader should be.[2]

We should learn how to ignore most offenses that come our way. For the annoyances that we cannot ignore, we should learn how to deflect them in a healthy way. For those matters that we ought not to ignore or deflect, we should confront them promptly, directly, and lovingly, all for the sake of reflecting Christ and preserving unity.

Lastly, we should be willing to fight for the heart of the faith—the truth of the gospel. We should be willing to fight for unity when unnecessary conflict rears its head. In order for us to be prepared for that, we have to continually remind ourselves of the truth of the gospel.[3] The biblical gospel is the good news that Christ willingly sacrificed Himself out of His immeasurable love for us. He did this to provide a once-and-for-all remedy for our sin, which alienates each of us from God. Christ has already done the work of our salvation; it has been accomplished. We do not earn God's love; He already demonstrated it definitively on the cross. We do not contribute to our salvation in any way other than placing our trust in Christ. We are saved by God's grace through our faith. Our whole life after salvation is one long journey of saying thank you to God with our lives and growing in Christlikeness.

That's the biblical gospel in a nutshell. Be on the lookout for distortions. Sometimes they're subtle, but they tend to show up in a few typical forms: *God doesn't really love me. I have to be a good person if I want God to like me. If I'm a Christian God is going to bless me with possessions, long life, or physical health. If things go wrong in my life, then I must have behaved badly or God doesn't really love me.* These thoughts reflect a misunderstanding of the gospel. The gospel is warped anytime we suggest that God doesn't love us or that our good behavior contributes to our salvation. The one true gospel is so counterintuitive that many of us in the church—to say nothing of the broader culture—have a hard time really believing it. We have to fight for the true gospel in our circles of influence, just as Paul did.

There are of course other conflicts that are worthwhile, which I won't enumerate here. A key takeaway from this chapter and Paul's ministry is that our list of things that are worth fighting about should be very short. I'll close with one final encouragement, once again from the insightful mind of Phillips: "Do what Lincoln did. Ignore most of the attacks if they are petty, but fight back when they are important enough to make a difference. . . . Maintain grace under pressure. Know right from wrong. And have courage."[4]

QUESTIONS FOR DISCUSSION/REFLECTION

- What stood out to you about this chapter?
- Have you ever picked a battle that you later realized was a mistake? How can you prevent a situation like that in the future?
- Do you have a coping mechanism to prevent unnecessary conflict like Abraham Lincoln's unsent letters?

- How do you know when the gospel is being threatened or distorted? What are some telltale signs?
- Why is unity so important in the church?
- What did you find most challenging about this chapter?
- What is one thing you can change this week based on what you learned in this chapter?
- Sample Prayer: God, I admit that I am too quick to engage in conflict. I acknowledge that when I feel criticized, my heart is often in the wrong place. My desire to justify or defend myself blinds me to the more important matters of unity, grace, and preserving relationships. Holy Spirit, please help me to respond to criticism the way You want me to. Help me to know which battles are worth fighting, and give me guidance on how to heal from the hurts that I'm not going to respond to. Lord Jesus, help me to remember that my identity and security is found in You and You alone. Father, give me the courage to engage in worthy conflict when necessary, and help me to do so in a manner that would bring You glory. Amen.

CHAPTER SIX

Genuine Collaboration

Finding Your Friends and Letting Them Lead

People will surprise you if you give them the chance to. That's a lesson I keep learning over and over again. It's amazing how many times I've underestimated people. I'm beginning to embrace the simple (yet strangely confounding) strategy of just plainly asking people for help—even people I think would never be interested in working together.

For example, I've had the opportunity to connect with secular organizations that help the poor. They are thrilled to partner with churches, even though their mission is not based explicitly on religious faith. They just want to help people, and in some cases they are better equipped than a local church to do so.

So often in the church we feel like we need to reinvent the wheel and create our own ministries from scratch, when our time, energy, and money might be better spent teaming up with another entity in the community that already has the lay of the land and has identified and addressed the fundamental challenges. We should be looking for organizations and individuals whose interests overlap with ours.

I've also been staggered by how eager brand-new Christians are to jump in and help with something substantial. That continues to surprise me for some reason. People are very willing to offer their gifts, time, and resources if you simply give them the chance to say yes. If you ask, they might say yes. If you don't ask, they definitely won't say yes.

For many people, helping a local church accomplish something is the very mechanism God uses to draw them into a relationship with Him. When the church can provide purpose and direction for a person's talents, a powerful connection is made. People get a taste of how God might want to use them to make the world a better place, and they usually want more.

When we were in the launch phase of Real Hope Community Church, we experienced this all the time. In addition to receiving support from ARC, we also received considerable assistance from other churches and people in our community. Some of the help came from families who were on our launch team; some came from those who were supportive but never joined our church. Some came from people who had little connection to us but just wanted to lend a helping hand. We had help with repairs to our trailer, setting up interest events, financial forecasting, researching the location of our portable church, configuring our software, running our lighting, engineering the way we pack our trailers, applying for our nonprofit status, managing our financial software, and planning events in our community. It was incredible the way God used friends and other organizations in the community to help us in our season of need.

When we look at Paul, we see a man who was perfectly willing to ask for help in major ways. It's hard to overstate the logistical and financial burdens of Paul's ministry. Travel was expensive, slow, and dangerous. Paul and his team sought to devote as much of their time as possible to preaching the gospel and shepherding the new congregations, but it was a challenge. They struggled to find venues where they could teach and safe places where they could lodge for lengthy periods. Paul and his team needed friends in the community to help them, and there were very few seasoned Christians at this point.

God orchestrated friendships for Paul with a handful of especially influential individuals, people who placed their trust in Christ and partnered with Paul in substantial ways. We will focus on three people like that in this chapter: the married couple Priscilla and Aquila, and a government official named Erastus. Paul worked alongside them for years and unleashed them for ministry.

COLLABORATION WITH PRISCILLA AND AQUILA

By the early 50s AD, Paul was becoming one of the most well-known voices in the fledgling Christian community, but after his split with Barnabas and Mark he had few friends he could rely on besides Silas, Timothy, and Luke. After Paul and company began their ministry in Europe, they made their way south through Greece, coming eventually to Corinth. It was there that he would meet Priscilla and Aquila, dear friends who would stick by his side for years.

Ancient Corinth was one of the most important cities in the Roman Empire. Because of its strategic location on a narrow isthmus, it had access to two important seaports—one facing west toward Italy, the other facing east toward the Aegean Sea. With this advantageous location, Corinth was a booming commercial center. It was so strategic, in fact, that the Roman Emperor Nero undertook the colossal task of carving a canal through the isthmus to further enable trade in that area.[1]

As we have seen, when Paul first arrived in a new town he often looked for a Jewish synagogue. Paul most likely met Priscilla and Aquila after connecting with the Jewish community in Corinth. In the book of Acts, we read about how they met:

> After this Paul left Athens and went to Corinth. And he found a Jew named Aquila, a native of Pontus, recently come from Italy with his wife Priscilla, because Claudius had commanded all the Jews to leave Rome. And he went to see them, and because he was of the same trade he stayed with them and worked, for they were tentmakers by trade. (Acts 18:1–3)

We learn some important things about Priscilla and Aquila from this passage. First, since Aquila was Jewish (and probably Priscilla, too), they would have had some familiarity with the Jewish Scriptures. Paul would have had common ground with this couple, and he may have been instrumental in them becoming committed followers of Christ.

Second, we learn that they were refugees. They had been living and working in Rome, and were kicked out of the city with the rest of the Jews by Emperor Claudius. This passage in Acts is corroborated by a Roman historian of the day named Suetonius. He wrote, "The Jews he expelled from Rome, since they were constantly in rebellion, at the instigation of Chrestus."[2] Scholars speculate about what exactly was going on in this episode, but they generally agree that Claudius expelled the Jews from Rome in the late 40s AD. Priscilla and Aquila had to pack up and head east to Corinth.

The text also tells us that Paul, Priscilla, and Aquila shared more than their Jewish cultural heritage: they were of the same trade. They were tentmakers, and they went into business together in Corinth. They may have had a shop on a street much like the one pictured below.

CORINTHIAN STREET WITH SHOP REMNANTS ON THE RIGHT.
PHOTO BY RYAN LOKKESMOE

The text also indicates that Paul lived with Priscilla and Aquila. When it says in verse 3 that Paul "stayed and worked with them," the Greek verb for *stayed* is almost always used by Luke to indicate lodging with someone.[3] Priscilla and Aquila seem to have helped Paul get on his feet in Corinth with both a job and a place to live.

But Priscilla and Aquila didn't just help Paul get established in Corinth; they were working alongside him in ministry for a significant period of time in that city. This is demonstrated by the fact that when Paul finally left and sailed east, Priscilla and Aquila accompanied him and took up residence in the metropolis of Ephesus: "Paul stayed many days longer and then took leave of the brothers and set sail for Syria, and with him Priscilla and Aquila. At Cenchreae he had cut his hair, for he was under a vow. And they came to Ephesus, and he left them there . . ." (Acts 18:18–19).

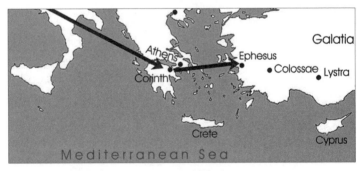

PRISCILLA AND AQUILA'S JOURNEY FROM ROME TO CORINTH TO EPHESUS

Paul apparently asked Priscilla and Aquila to stay in Ephesus and help with the new Christian community in that city, because a little later in the same chapter we see them getting to know the influential traveling teacher Apollos (and straightening out his theology):

> Now a Jew named Apollos, a native of Alexandria, came to Ephesus. He was an eloquent man, competent in the Scriptures. He had been instructed in the way of the Lord. And being fervent in spirit, he spoke and taught accurately the things concerning Jesus, though he knew only the baptism of John. He began to speak boldly in the synagogue, but when Priscilla and Aquila heard him, they took him aside and explained to him the way of God more accurately. (Acts 18:24–26)

Priscilla and Aquila came from Rome, settled in Corinth, where they lived and worked with Paul, and then relocated *again* to Ephesus, where they continued their ministry. To Paul, they were indispensable friends and ministry partners. With that mention of Priscilla and Aquila, they drop out of the narrative in the book of Acts.

However, Priscilla and Aquila are mentioned a handful of other times in the New Testament—each time by Paul in one of his letters. The most obvious difference we observe in Paul's letters is that he refers to Priscilla by her more formal name, Prisca.[4]

The earliest mention we have of the couple is at the end of 1 Corinthians, written sometime in the mid-50s AD. When Paul wrote the letter, he was no longer in the city of Corinth, but had moved east to Ephesus and was writing back to the church in Corinth, which he served for more than eighteen months. From Ephesus, he wrote, "The churches of Asia send you greetings. Aquila and Prisca, together with the church in their house, send you hearty greetings in the Lord" (1 Cor. 16:19).

As we saw in the Acts account, Priscilla and Aquila followed Paul to Ephesus and began to work in ministry there. When Paul wrote to his Christian brothers and sisters back in Corinth, he made sure to mention that Priscilla and Aquila said hello. Most of the recipients would have known who they were. He also mentioned in this letter that Priscilla and Aquila had a church that met in their house in Ephesus. This is clear evidence that they were financially well off. Relatively few people in the Roman Empire had the means to own a home that could accommodate a church gathering.

The next mention of Priscilla and Aquila is found in Romans 16:3–5, written a few years later in the late 50s AD. Paul writes, "Greet Prisca and Aquila, my fellow workers in Christ Jesus, who risked their necks for my life, to whom not only I give thanks but all the churches of the Gentiles give thanks as well. Greet also the church in their house" (Rom. 16:3–5).

This passage tells us a few interesting things. First of all, Priscilla and Aquila were not with Paul anymore. Paul was probably writing from Corinth to Rome, where Priscilla and Aquila were allowed to live again. Paul was asking the Roman Christians to say hello to Priscilla and Aquila for him. Second, Paul called Priscilla and Aquila his "fellow workers." As we noted earlier, this *syn-* prefix word was a common expression Paul used for his true partners in ministry. Not only were Priscilla and Aquila Paul's fellow workers, according to this passage they risked their lives for him. They had demonstrated their commitment to him and a willingness to suffer for the gospel of Christ.

Finally, we learn that a church was meeting in their house in Rome. It appears that Priscilla and Aquila had used their multi-city business to support Paul and the ministry, and were now hosting a church in their home in the Roman imperial capital. Owning a home would have been very expensive in the incredibly dense urban center of Rome. Most average people would have lived in tiny, poorly ventilated apartment blocks. Having a home with adequate space to host a church would have been quite a luxury for the Christian community in the capital.

We are now beginning to get a sense of just how affluent Priscilla and Aquila were. They had homes in at least three major cities (Rome, Corinth, and Ephesus), and we know for sure that the homes were large enough to host a church in at least two locations (Rome and Ephesus). It is probable that they had a similar living situation in Corinth, though we have no direct evidence of that. All we know is that Paul stayed with them. Added to this, the ease with which Priscilla and Aquila moved back and forth between these cities indicates how wealthy they were. That sort of flexibility and stability was almost always associated with wealth in the ancient world.

The last time we hear about Priscilla and Aquila is when Paul mentioned them at the end of his final letter, 2 Timothy, written sometime in the mid-60s AD. Paul was imprisoned in Rome awaiting his trial when he wrote it, and it is clear from the letter that he knew his death was near. Priscilla and Aquila were probably in Ephesus, because it is likely that Timothy (the recipient of this letter) was leading the church in that city. In the last few verses of the letter, Paul wrote, "Greet Prisca and Aquila, and the household of Onesiphorus" (2 Tim. 4:19).

In Paul's final letter, Priscilla and Aquila were two of the last names he ever mentioned. Their friendship and partnership in Paul's ministry through the years had been invaluable, and he wanted to make sure to say goodbye to his old friends.

What shape would Paul's ministry have taken if he had not sought out the friendship of people like Priscilla and Aquila, and unleashed them for ministry? It's hard to imagine their absence. Now let's look at another influential friend on Paul's team, who hailed from Corinth.

COLLABORATION WITH ERASTUS

Erastus is mentioned only three times in the New Testament. He served in Paul's ministry, and in Romans 16:23 Paul describes him as the "city treasurer" of Corinth. The title *city treasurer* is a translation of a word Paul used: οἰκονόμος (*oikonomos*). This word usually refers to a government official, often a treasurer.[5] The English word *economy* comes from this Greek word, which has to do with household management.

Thus, Erastus was something like the city treasurer of Corinth, one of the most prosperous cities in the Roman world. In the public sphere he would have been an onstage leader, but he seems to have played some sort of offstage role in the Christian community. We get a small clue in Acts 19:22:

"And having sent into Macedonia two of his helpers, Timothy and Erastus, [Paul] himself stayed in Asia for a while."

The phrase *two of his helpers* is more literally translated "two of those who were helping him" (or "ministering to him"). The word we translate as *help* is διακονέω (*diakoneō*), which means, "to serve, wait on; care for, see after, provide for."[6] Erastus, it seems, was someone whose life was oriented around serving the apostle Paul in his ministry. He truly partnered with him. The picture from Acts is that Paul sent Erastus from Corinth in southern Greece up to Macedonia in northern Greece. This prestigious government official joined Paul's team and prioritized it so highly that he ended up leaving his home to serve the needs of the ministry.[7]

I have a good story about Erastus, if you'll indulge me. There is only one time in my life when I have felt like Indiana Jones, and it was because of Erastus. In grad school I read about an inscription in Corinth that referred to Erastus. It's rare to find the name of someone from the New Testament etched in first-century stone, so I wanted to see it.[8] When my wife, Ashley, and I took a trip to Greece and Turkey right after I finished my PhD coursework, Corinth was on the itinerary—and I was thrilled. I wanted to walk the streets where Paul did ministry with Priscilla and Aquila, the place where they worked together as tentmakers. I wanted to see with my own eyes the city that received the letters we call 1 and 2 Corinthians. And I wanted to find the Erastus inscription.

When we arrived in Corinth with our tour group, I was amazed at the natural beauty of the setting and how well-preserved the ancient city was. As we followed our tour guide around, it became clear she was more interested in telling us stories from Greek mythology than explaining the history of what we were seeing. I was getting antsy. I hadn't seen the Erastus inscription anywhere, so I left our tour group and walked back to the main entrance.

I found a few employees working at the ticket booth by the entrance and clumsily asked, "Erastus?" These were not archaeologists, and it's safe to say they had no idea what I was talking about. I explained that I was looking for a name written on a road, but I couldn't find it. They understood that I was looking for something I hadn't found in the main touristy area, so they pointed across the street. When I walked over there, I discovered that there was more of Ancient Corinth to explore—but this part of the city was not part of the official tour. It was an overgrown section of the ancient city, with streets and structures partially exposed.

I climbed down the steep hill and found myself standing on an ancient paved street. I walked along it and found the crumbling remains of an old amphitheater.

I hadn't seen anything and was starting to worry that the tour bus might leave me behind, so I began to head back. And then I saw it: the Erastus inscription by the side of the ancient road! I quickly took some pictures, climbed back up the hill, ran across the street, shouted a quick thank you to the ticket booth employees, and found Ashley. Then we ran back across the street together, down the hill, and I showed her what I saw:

It is probable that this inscription referred to the same Erastus mentioned by Paul in his letters and by Luke in the book of Acts, because it is dated to the mid-first century. The inscription, written in Latin, reads "Erastus in return for the aedileship paved it [the pavement adjoining the theatre] at

his own expense."[9] The Latin title *Aedile* approximates the Greek word that Paul used to describe Erastus (*oikonomos*). The Aedile of Corinth was "a city business manager responsible for such property as streets, public buildings and markets, as well as for the revenue gleaned from them. He was also a judge who decided most of the city's commercial and financial litigation."[10] This fits with what we know of Erastus.

As *aedile/oikonomos* of Corinth, Erastus was a man of considerable power and influence. He had enough wealth to personally finance the paving of a street in a city that he helped to govern, a street that Paul, Priscilla, and Aquila routinely walked upon. He used his position, administrative skills, and financial resources in service of the church in a time when it was very unpopular and sometimes dangerous to be a Christian. He rearranged his life in service of the gospel.

When Paul first came to Corinth, it wasn't clear how the city would respond. Most of the Jewish community rejected his message, but God had plans for that city:

> The Lord said to Paul one night in a vision, "Do not
> be afraid, but go on speaking and do not be silent,
> for I am with you, and no one will attack you to harm
> you, for I have many in this city who are my people."
> And he stayed a year and six months, teaching the
> word of God among them. (Acts 18:9–11)

I have to imagine that Priscilla, Aquila, and Erastus were some of the people that God had in mind when He said He had many in Corinth who were His. Paul stayed there a year and a half, and it must have been so helpful and encouraging to be friends with influential people in the community: Priscilla and Aquila in the business sector, Erastus in the government.[11] They gave of their financial resources, their time, their emotional energy, and their homes. All three of them ended up leaving Corinth as members of Paul's team in order to share Christ with the world.

WHAT THIS MEANS FOR US TODAY

We can learn a lot about leadership and influence from this Corinthian trio. This is a great example of reciprocal influence: Paul influenced Priscilla, Aquila, and Erastus spiritually, and they in turn influenced the shape of his ministry by the resources and opportunities they could provide. Paul was humble enough to accept their help and partner with them in a substantial way. They were humble enough to let this traveling preacher from Tarsus speak into their lives and give them a new gospel-shaped purpose. Paul influenced them, and they influenced Paul. Their influence was mutual. They were a team.

In the same way, we who are in ministry leadership need to be real about our needs and ask for help from those in our community who can help us—even if they're not exactly mature Christians yet. We need to remember that for many people, the use of their gifts and resources might be their path back to the church (or to Christ in the first place). We must be willing to find and empower these people for leadership in key roles, because God can use them powerfully to open doors, as he did with Priscilla, Aquila, and Erastus. Remember, Paul would have spent months or years apart from these people as he continued to travel and spread the gospel to new territories. He left them behind without real-time oversight. He showed a lot of trust in them.

There may also be partners *outside* the church—though I have sensed most Christians are hesitant to explore this. There is an incongruity here that hinders our ability to find our friends in the community the way that Paul seemed to. On the one hand, we have a genuine love and concern for those who are unconnected to the church. We think about them, pray for them, serve them, and reach out to them. We care deeply for those individuals who have not yet responded to God's grace or who have drifted away from the church.

And yet, many of us simultaneously embrace a culture-war mentality toward those same people as a *group*. We feel threatened by "the culture" and the way we feel it is attacking Christian values. It seems we have forgotten that this monolithic, impersonal "culture" is made up of the same individuals we care so much about and design our ministries to reach. It's a tragic and debilitating contradiction.

One of the by-products of this outlook is that those of us in the Christian community often feel like we need to go it alone. We presume, perhaps unconsciously, that the only people who would want to help us in our ministries are other Christians. So we turn a blind eye to community leaders and organizations whose missions might overlap with ours. We make the assumption that people who don't yet know Jesus would never be interested in helping us.

We in the church need to be better at finding people who can help us—people who might have a better idea than we do about how to strategically reach an area for Christ. We need to get to know our local government officials, police and fire chiefs, school board members, principals, prominent business owners, and real estate agents—regardless of whether or not they're Christians—because some of them might be our future Priscillas. Our Aquilas. Our Erastuses. We need to invite them into our world and sincerely ask for their help—not in a condescending way that suggests we know the best type of help they can offer. We need to genuinely and transparently admit our need for their assistance, while helping them grasp that God might have a higher purpose for their time and resources.

Some of you reading this chapter, however, are not the Paul in the story. You are a Priscilla. You are an Aquila. You are an Erastus. You own a business, run a school, or serve on an influential government committee. You have a type of influence in the community that the church does not have. You can open doors that ministry leaders never could. If that's you, I encourage you to finish this chapter and immediately email a pastor. Let them know what you do for a living, and that you'd like to help the ministry in whatever way you can. Schedule a lunch or coffee and just start a conversation. You never know what God might want to do through a partnership between you and local church leadership.

Make it easy on your pastor. Initiate this conversation. If you don't get around to it, and your pastor is the one who initiates, then I encourage you to enthusiastically accept. Let your pastor show you a spiritual trajectory for your influence, and show your pastor a way to impact the community in partnership with you.

Church leaders: find your friends in the community. Show the courage to look for them in unexpected places, and the humility to be influenced by them even as you are providing leadership. If you are not on a church staff, use your influence to be a friend to the local church leaders. Enter into ministry partnership together. Be fellow workers like Paul was with Priscilla and Aquila. Trust each other and trust God. That's what Paul and his team did, and so should we.

QUESTIONS FOR DISCUSSION/REFLECTION

- What stood out to you about this chapter?
- Why do you think churches are reluctant to partner with people and entities outside of the church?
- What are the risks of entrusting leadership to new believers? What are some benefits?
- What skills or resources do you have that you might be able to offer to the local church?
- What is one problem you see in your community that could be effectively addressed with a partnership between a local church and another organization?
- What did you find most challenging about this chapter?
- What is one thing you can change this week based on what you learned in this chapter?
- Sample Prayer: Lord God, I want to see people the way You do. I want to see their God-given potential, even if they don't. Help me to be someone who reaches out into the community to make friendships and discover partnerships—in the same way that Paul and his team did. I realize that my family background and church

experiences probably make it easy for me to make assumptions about people. I don't want to do that. Please rid me of any attitude that might presume certain people are beyond Your reach. Amen.

CHAPTER SEVEN

Kingdom Diplomacy

Building Bridges across Cultural Chasms

I magine a crowded room full of people shouting at each other—a tumultuous scene. People are struggling to be heard, defending themselves, attacking others, and pushing people out of the way. It's a room full of grieved people airing their grievances; hurt people hurting each other. They have very different reasons for their anger. Some feel they have been wounded by someone else in the room. Others are angry at the insinuation that they did anything wrong. Some are upset that they even have to be in the room in the first place. Everyone has different explanations for how the argument got started, and no one can imagine it ever ending. There doesn't seem to be an exit. It's a painful, fractured melee that everyone sees differently, and it just keeps going.

In many ways, that room is our world. We experience that room on social media, in our communities, in the realm of local and geopolitics, and in our workplaces. Sometimes, our families feel like that room. However hopeless it might seem, we Christians need to be in that room because we bring hope with us. The church should stand together and do the hard work of peacemaking and reconciliation. We should be helping others to listen, and see the best in each other. We are meant to be living examples of countercultural grace. That's our voice. That's how Christians should sound in a world that is wired for discord.

The church is in the business of restoration and bridge-building because Jesus was about those things. That much is obvious from a plain reading of the Gospels. Sadly, true restoration is rare within the church. Too often our posture is divisive, judgmental, and self-justifying. But that's not who we Christians are meant to be. We are meant to be envoys for reconciliation, diplomats of the kingdom. Or, as Paul put it in 2 Corinthians 5:20, "We are ambassadors for Christ, God making his appeal through us."

While we are indeed called to use our influence to seek peace in personal conflicts, this chapter will not address interpersonal divisions. We will instead focus here on structural or systemic divisions: chasms in our culture that perpetuate resentment and make reconciliation seem out of reach.

In the name of Christ we are called to bridge social boundaries like race and socioeconomic status. We are meant to reach across the chasms of gender and political philosophy. We are charged with navigating stark differences of language, nationality, and worldview in such a way that we can find friendship on the other side of division. We are called to help restore trust and goodwill between those separated by any sort of ideological divide—whether they believe in God or not. Our responsibility is not only toward those of faith. We must never forget that we represent Christ to a world that is watching.

Paul and his team left us a wonderful example in the way they handled a particularly painful and seemingly insurmountable cultural challenge. One of the great ironies of Paul's writing career is that the biggest social rift in the early church was dealt with in his shortest and most overlooked letter: Philemon.

THE CIRCUMSTANCES
BEHIND PAUL'S LETTER TO PHILEMON

In the early 60s AD, Paul was in prison in Rome, pastoring remote congregations via letter and his leadership team. He was prayerfully guiding a loose confederation of young churches through social tensions, leadership challenges, government pressure, and a number of other destabilizing forces. It was a heavy burden of leadership, especially for someone suffering imprisonment.

Paul and his team were working to create unity in a highly stratified, racist, power-oriented society. In fact, one cannot adequately understand the world of the New Testament without understanding that it was a world obsessed with power, honor, and dominance. The Roman legions took control and maintained it through brute force. The richest members of society grasped on to power and wealth and presided over a system that kept almost everyone else poor and subjugated.

Men in Roman households—known as the *paterfamilias*

—governed their homes in most cases as autocrats. They were the unquestioned rulers of their households. Then you had the millions of slaves, who not only lacked wealth, but also the dignity of being considered human. *Nothing* in the Roman world was geared toward unity or leveling the playing field. This is the world in which the gospel of Jesus Christ—a truly countercultural message—first began to spread. Imagine Paul speaking these words into that sort of climate: "There is neither Jew nor Greek, there is neither slave nor free, there is no male and female, for you are all one in Christ Jesus" (Gal. 3:28).

The division between slave and free was the biggest and most visible social boundary in the Roman Empire. It is estimated that somewhere between 20–50 percent of the inhabitants of cities were slaves. On one occasion, there was a proposal in the Roman Senate to require slaves to dress differently than the rest of the population. The proposal was ultimately abandoned because the senators did not want the slaves to know how numerous they were.[1] Most slaves during the time of the New Testament were born into slavery, because people who were born to slave mothers were automatically slaves. There was also a profitable slave trade that operated throughout the Empire.

Slaves were generally viewed as less than a person, sometimes being referred to in the ancient literature with dehumanizing terms like "articulate instruments" or "things with the feet of a man."[2] They were often given demeaning names like Felix, which meant "lucky." The particular slave we will discuss in this chapter had a similarly condescending name. More on that in a moment.

Most slaves lived their daily lives under the threat of

physical punishment, and they had to cope with all sorts of emotional abuse. They were under the total control of their master, with zero legal protections, and probably experienced the sale of family members or friends with no expectation of ever seeing them again. Many slaves even experienced sexual abuse by their masters, which was considered socially acceptable in most cases. The life of a slave was full of pain and devoid of hope.

In my PhD work, I took a special interest in the social world of the New Testament, and I found myself particularly interested in this issue of slavery within first-century Christianity. That interest led me to write my dissertation on the historical backdrop of Paul's letter to Philemon. It's not surprising that the letter is neglected, because it's so short (only 335 words in Greek). In most printed Bibles, it only takes up about half of a page. The letter also requires an unusual amount of background knowledge to fully appreciate, so its relevance to our modern lives isn't as obvious as some of Paul's other writings.

But if we take the time to understand what's going on in that letter, it's one of the most powerful case studies I'm aware of when it comes to understanding Christian influence. The story behind Paul's letter to Philemon involves three people:

(1) **The apostle Paul**, who is imprisoned and awaiting trial in Rome.
(2) **Philemon**, a wealthy Christian man from the town of Colossae who hosts a church in his home. (Colossae was near Ephesus in modern Turkey, hundreds of miles from Rome where Paul was incarcerated.)

(3) **Onesimus**, a fugitive slave who ran away from the house of Philemon.

Here's what happened in a nutshell: Onesimus was a slave in Philemon's household. Because of some conflict he had with his master (or perhaps because of a general longing for freedom), Onesimus ran away. This was a perilous choice, because fugitive slaves were routinely tortured or killed if they were caught. It is probable that Onesimus had to steal from Philemon in order to finance his flight. Roman law required people to turn in fugitives if they were discovered, so it is likely that there were professional slave catchers, or even Philemon's own people, looking for Onesimus.

Eventually Onesimus made his way to Rome, where he found the imprisoned apostle Paul. The journey would have taken months, if not longer. Scholars debate whether Onesimus fled with the intention of finding Paul and asking for his help in reconciling with Philemon.[3] We are not sure how long Onesimus was with Paul in Rome, but we know that he became a Christian there as a result of Paul's influence.

The letter to Philemon in our New Testament was Paul's attempt to reconcile Onesimus and Philemon. Fugitive slave and Christian master. Let's look at what Paul wrote and—more importantly—*how* he wrote it. It's a brilliantly diplomatic letter and we can learn a lot from it as we think about bridging sensitive social divides. Because the content of Philemon is so rich and dense, I'll walk through it in sections and offer some brief comments along the way. Stick with me—there is a wealth of valuable insight in this short letter.

PAUL'S DIPLOMACY WITH PHILEMON

Paul begins with a fairly typical address:

> Paul, a prisoner for Christ Jesus, and Timothy our
> brother, To Philemon our beloved fellow worker
> and Apphia our sister and Archippus our fellow
> soldier, and the church in your house: Grace to you
> and peace from God our Father and the Lord Jesus
> Christ. (Philem. 1–3)

At the very beginning of the letter, Paul is already beginning his diplomatic work. When Philemon read this letter, he would have known right at the beginning that both Paul and Timothy are aware of it, since Timothy is listed as a co-sender. Furthermore, Paul addressed the letter to Apphia and Archippus in addition to Philemon (who may have been his family), and he also instructed the letter be read to the church that meets in Philemon's home. Thus, Paul is alerting Philemon to the fact that there are two Christian communities listening in to what he's about to write. The difficult subject matter of the letter will be handled in a climate of accountability. It may be a personal letter, but it will be read publicly and Philemon's response will be observed.

Paul continues,

> I thank my God always when I remember you in my
> prayers, because I hear of your love and of the faith
> that you have toward the Lord Jesus and for all the
> saints, and I pray that the sharing of your faith may

become effective for the full knowledge of every
good thing that is in us for the sake of Christ. For I
have derived much joy and comfort from your love,
my brother, because the hearts of the saints have
been refreshed through you. (Philem. 4–7)

Here Paul expresses his affection and admiration for Philemon. He praises Philemon for his spiritual maturity and
the example he sets for others, and Paul lets him know how
much he personally appreciates his leadership. This passage
serves two intertwined purposes: Paul genuinely expresses
his respect for Philemon, while simultaneously softening
him up for the difficult subject matter that is about to follow.
Paul is carefully setting a tone—doing what he can to disarm
Philemon.

Having done so, Paul broaches the Onesimus subject:

Accordingly, though I am bold enough in Christ to
command you to do what is required, yet for love's
sake I prefer to appeal to you—I, Paul, an old man
and now a prisoner also for Christ Jesus—I appeal to
you for my child, Onesimus, whose father I became
in my imprisonment. (Formerly he was useless to
you, but now he is indeed useful to you and to me.) I
am sending him back to you, sending my very heart.
I would have been glad to keep him with me, in
order that he might serve me on your behalf during
my imprisonment for the gospel, but I preferred to
do nothing without your consent in order that your
goodness might not be by compulsion but of your

own accord. For this perhaps is why he was parted from you for a while, that you might have him back forever, no longer as a bondservant but more than a bondservant, as a beloved brother—especially to me, but how much more to you, both in the flesh and in the Lord. (Philem. 8–16)

With verse 8 Paul gets to the point, and he does so in a masterful way. He insinuates that as an apostle he *could* order Philemon to comply with the request that he is about to make, but he doesn't want to have to play that card. He instead appeals to Philemon's character, which he has already commended in the first part of the letter. Paul also reminds Philemon that he is an old man in prison, hoping, it seems, that this would elicit sympathy and further soften Philemon's posture toward his request.

Then in verse 10 Paul refers to Onesimus by name for the first time in the letter. Knowing that even the mention of his name would probably provoke Philemon, Paul introduces Onesimus as his spiritual child, a designation he typically used for those he led to Christ. To break the anticipated tension at this point, Paul follows with a pun. The name Onesimus means "useful," and Paul uses a play on words to say that Onesimus has been *truly* useful to him in service of the gospel. Paul calls Onesimus "[his] very heart"—additional affectionate language designed to produce sympathy in Philemon.

Next, Paul tells Philemon that he wants Onesimus to stay in Rome and continue his valuable work in the ministry, but only if Philemon freely allows it. With this, he gives Philemon a clear opportunity to choose to do the Christlike thing. Philemon would not have that choice if Paul didn't send Onesimus back. Paul is not disputing that Philemon has certain legal rights as a slave owner; he is calling him to willingly lay down those rights.

Then, in the most revolutionary moment in the letter, Paul suggests that Philemon cease to view Onesimus as a slave, and instead view him as a brother in Christ. Paul seems to imply that it might have been by divine providence that Onesimus came to Rome in the first place ("this perhaps is why he was parted from you for a while . . ."). Paul continues:

> So if you consider me your partner, receive him as you would receive me. If he has wronged you at all, or owes you anything, charge that to my account. I, Paul, write this with my own hand: I will repay it— to say nothing of your owing me even your own self. Yes, brother, I want some benefit from you in the Lord. Refresh my heart in Christ. Confident of your obedience, I write to you, knowing that you will do even more than I say. At the same time, prepare a guest room for me, for I am hoping that through your prayers I will be graciously given to you. (Philem. 17–22)

Paul tactfully raises the stakes in this section. He asks Philemon to treat Onesimus not as a runaway slave, but as the apostle himself. Then, Paul removes any financial reason that might cause Philemon reluctance; if Onesimus did in fact steal from Philemon in order to finance his flight (which is probable), Paul is personally offering to repay that debt.

The fact that he wrote the letter with his own hand makes this section a *de facto* IOU. Then, in the most confrontational moment of the letter, Paul reminds Philemon of the great spiritual debt he owes to the apostle. In case that was too harsh, Paul follows with another pun, saying that he wants some "benefit" in the Lord from Philemon (the word *benefit* in Greek sounds like the name Onesimus).

Paul expresses his confidence that Philemon will do the right thing, but can't help but offer one more subtle pressure point: letting Philemon know that he hopes to visit in person soon. Paul wraps up the letter with a few personal greetings, which served the purpose of once again reinforcing that there were many people aware of the letter: "Epaphras, my fellow prisoner in Christ Jesus, sends greetings to you, and so do Mark, Aristarchus, Demas, and Luke, my fellow workers. The grace of the Lord Jesus Christ be with your spirit" (Philem. 23–25).

That's the whole letter. Paul's approach is an education in how Christian influencers should approach divisive issues. Paul was thoughtful. He advocated for the person at a social disadvantage by helping the more powerful party develop Christlike empathy. Paul was nuanced. He did not indulge in a simplistic culture-war mentality. He lovingly spoke truth into a volatile situation. Paul found a way to be disarming while also holding Philemon accountable. He affirmed Philemon, elevated Onesimus, and helped them both to see that their shared identity in Christ was the only identity category that mattered.

Paul's letter to Philemon is a historical gem, because it's the only letter we have of Paul's in which we get to observe him practicing what he preaches. For the most part he's preaching in his other letters. In this one, we are like a fly on the wall observing Paul address a real challenge. We see him applying what he teaches in Galatians 3:28: "There is neither Jew nor Greek, there is neither slave nor free, there is no male and female, for you are all one in Christ Jesus." Paul teaches us and—in the case of Philemon—*shows* us that we Christians are supposed to demolish cultural boundaries in the name of Christ.

WHAT THIS MEANS FOR US TODAY

There was no shortage of opportunities for Paul and his team to confront social rifts that had no place in the church. For example, in Ephesians 2 Paul addressed the ancient cultural barrier between Jews and Gentiles by referring to a physical wall that separated them during Jesus' lifetime. In the Jerusalem Temple, there was a well-known stone barrier that separated the massive outer courts from the inner temple where the worship and sacrifices took place. This wall in the temple was constructed to separate the Jews from the Gentiles. If you were a Jew, you could go past the barrier into the temple proper. In effect, you could get close to God.

If you were a Gentile, however, you could not go past the barrier. In fact, when you approached the wall you would have noticed warning signs indicating that you would be immediately killed if you dared to go past it. Ancient writers outside of the Bible described this wall in the temple, and archaeologists have discovered two of the wall's warning signs. This was the text of the warning:

No man of another nation is to enter within the barrier and enclosure around the temple. Whoever is caught will have himself to blame for his death which follows.[4]

If you were a Gentile, a wall separated you from the Jews and kept you away from God's presence. Division and distance were physically manifested in stone, propped up in the temple for thousands of people to see on a daily basis. But then Jesus came along, and the wall lost its power to divide. Paul referred to this physical wall to make a theological point about Christ's uniting work on the cross: "But now in Christ Jesus you who once were far off have been brought near by the blood of Christ. For he himself is our peace, who has made us both one and has broken down in his flesh the *dividing wall* of hostility" (Eph. 2:13–14). Because of Christ, Jews and Gentiles could now worship God together in the church. That wall became irrelevant.

However, some barriers are not made of brick and mortar. They are made of something more durable: social norms. In the case of his letter to Philemon, Paul was trying to knock down the cultural barricade between slave and free, and he had many other occasions in his ministry to punch holes in the barriers between rich and poor, Jews and Gentiles, and men and women. We are called to do the same.

If we are to be the Christian influencers God calls us to be, we need to have an eye for the seams in the social fabric of our communities. We must look for the fraying edges of that fabric, and then be the voices of reconciliation. We should lift up the low and give a loving perspective to the high. We need to follow Paul's example and not see things as simplistic or too clear-cut. We ought to avoid seeing one group as all wrong and the other as all right. We need to avoid unwittingly affirming divisions in our communities by not speaking out or by viewing them as the product of insurmountable problems. And we definitely need to become aware of how our modern political allegiances may be hindering our efforts in this area or shaping our rhetoric in unproductive ways. We must become the relentless voices of grace and unity in the name of Christ.

After Paul wrote his letter to Philemon, he asked Onesimus to carry it back to Philemon in Colossae. Tychicus went with him. When Onesimus arrived in Colossae months later, the community would have been shocked. Fugitive slaves rarely returned to their masters willingly.

We don't have a historical record of how Philemon reacted to the return of Onesimus, but the very fact that Paul's short letter survived and made it into the New Testament suggests that Philemon responded positively. If Philemon didn't follow Paul's leadership, he probably would have gotten rid of the letter. Philemon may have allowed Onesimus to return to Rome and serve with Paul on his behalf, still as his slave. It's also possible that Philemon went as far as freeing Onesimus as a result of Paul's letter. We do not know for sure; we only know what Paul hoped would happen.[5]

We as Christian leaders need to adopt the lovingly diplomatic posture that Paul exhibited in his letter to Philemon, and collectively apply our influence to the arduous task of smashing cultural barriers and building bridges of reconciliation. If we don't, who will? If the rest of the world sings most often in the key of discord, then we Christians must sing in a different key.

QUESTIONS FOR DISCUSSION/REFLECTION

- What stood out to you about this chapter?
- Have you ever read Philemon before? What did you notice about it when reading this chapter?
- What cultural chasms do you see in your community? How is the local church involved, and how can you help?
- How does the act of bridging cultural divides represent Christ to the community?
- Read Paul's letter to Philemon again (it's only 25 verses). What do you notice after reading it a second time?
- What did you find most challenging about this chapter?
- What is one thing you can change this week based on what you learned in this chapter?
- Sample Prayer: Lord Jesus, I want to be a voice of reconciliation and unity in the spheres of influence You have entrusted to me. Help me to see the chasms that need to be bridged. Show me the ways that I can be a voice of healing. Show me the social wounds in my community, and give me the courage to lovingly address them. Help me to endure the inevitable criticism that will come my way, and to not be deterred by it. I trust You to do the real work of healing—I am Your servant. Amen.

CHAPTER EIGHT

Relational Stewardship

Making People Feel Visible and Valued

Have you ever gotten a personal, encouraging note from a pastor or mentor? How did it make you feel to know that they remembered and valued you? I have received several letters or emails like that over the years, and they are always life-giving. I can remember verbatim phrases in several of them, and I haven't looked at them in years.

Great influencers make people feel visible and valued. Abraham Lincoln did this. He did not sequester himself in the marbled halls of the White House. He took the time to respond personally to letters from average people on relatively inconsequential topics. He received visitors who had minor grievances compared to the scope of the horrific Civil War that was going on. Lincoln got to know the troops and the staff working in the telegraph office at the War Department. He made it a point to ask about their well-being, and he remembered their names.

This sort of personal touch won over many people, even Lincoln's most ardent detractors.

One of the fundamental premises of this book is that Paul operated within a team, a group of people that has become mostly invisible to us over the centuries. He was not a lone ranger. In our minds, however, Paul has gotten most—if not all—of the leadership credit for the growth of his ministry, even though he himself continually deflected praise and highlighted the important contributions of others. It is understandable that we would give him an outsized share of credit, considering he was an apostle and that he authored most of the letters we read in the New Testament. It is undisputed that Paul was uniquely called by Christ and set aside for an especially fruitful ministry.

Yet there is a simple and easily remedied reason why we focus so singularly on Paul: we skip over the places in his letters where he went out of his way to make his team visible. In an effort to focus on the more universally relevant content of Paul's writings, we skim (or ignore) the beginnings and ends of his letters, which are deep reservoirs of insight relating to his team and their relationships. There is much to learn there, so we will focus on those sections in this chapter.

Paul's letters generally followed a fairly consistent structure, with minor variations depending on the needs of the individual letter:

- Salutation
- Thanksgiving
- Blessing
- Body of the letter

- Personal greetings
- Signature
- Closing benediction[1]

The main areas we tend to ignore are the opening salutation, commendations, and personal greetings. They're easy to ignore because their relevance to our lives is not obvious. Those are the moments when the letter takes on a decisively historical character, reminding us they were written two thousand years ago in another cultural context. "Who are these people?" we ask ourselves when we come to these sections. And then we skip over them, believing them not to be applicable to our twenty-first-century lives.

However, understanding why these sections are in our Bible will help us see that they are indeed relevant. Travel and communication in the Roman world was slow, arduous, and expensive. In his insightful article "The Holy Internet: Communication between Churches in the First Christian Generation," Michael Thompson gives us a glimpse of what the communication looked like:

> The holy internet hummed with traffic for many reasons. Travel was a necessity for a wide variety of people including merchants, freedmen in pursuit of new jobs, letter carriers, artisans, actors, athletes, runaway slaves, teachers, students, the sick seeking mineral springs and places for healing, government officials, soldiers, and tourists to see the sights . . . the holy internet hungered for news. [The Christians']

shared commitment in love and their sense of
community as God's family naturally led Christians
to desire information about how brothers and sisters
were faring.[2]

The fledgling Christian community depended on regular
communiqués from distant leaders and congregations, and it
required a lot of time, money, energy, and sacrifice to assure
such regular communication. That being the case, Paul was
diligent to include not only teaching content in his letters,
but important personal and social information that fostered
community and relationships within the growing network of
churches. It was vital for him to include that information. It
should be important to us as well.

We will now look together at some examples of Pauline
salutations, commendations, and greetings. In each case, I
will draw attention to the individuals mentioned, and then
the descriptive words Paul used for these people. (The names
will be in bold, the descriptions underlined.) These are the
moments when Paul highlighted his team members and the
nature of their relationships. I will make some brief comments below each text, and then draw some broader conclusions afterwards about all of them and how they impact the
way we view our role as influencers.

RELATIONSHIPS IN SALUTATIONS

Paul and **Timothy**, <u>servants</u> of Christ Jesus, To all
the saints in Christ Jesus who are at Philippi, with

the **overseers** and **deacons**: Grace to you and peace from God our Father and the Lord Jesus Christ. (Phil. 1:1–2)

Notice how Paul includes Timothy as a co-sender, and describes both of them as "servants"—a humble designation that reflects Jesus' picture of leaders as servants. Paul addresses the letter to "the saints" (literally "holy ones") in Philippi, and then highlights the leadership structure there, honoring and legitimizing the "overseers" and "deacons" who served that community.

Let's consider another salutation:

Paul, a prisoner for Christ Jesus, and **Timothy** our brother, To **Philemon** our beloved fellow worker and **Apphia** our sister and **Archippus** our fellow soldier, and the **church in your house**: Grace to you and peace from God our Father and the Lord Jesus Christ. (Philem. 1–3)

Remarkably, Paul does not call himself an apostle here or use some sort of title to establish his credibility. He identifies himself as a "prisoner," drawing attention to his humble circumstances. He co-sends the letter with Timothy, whom he calls "our brother," communicating both affection ("brother") and also community ("our"). There are three individual addressees, whom Paul encourages with the descriptive words he applies to them. Philemon is a "beloved fellow worker." Apphia is "our sister." Archippus is "our fellow soldier." This communal, familial language was intended to make them feel valued. Paul also includes the church that meets in Philemon's home, so they get to observe this interaction and the warmth it conveys.

RELATIONSHIPS IN COMMENDATIONS

> I commend to you <u>our sister</u> **Phoebe**, a <u>servant</u> of the church at Cenchreae, that you may welcome her in the Lord in a way worthy of the saints, and help her in whatever she may need from you, for she has been a <u>patron</u> of many and of myself as well. (Rom. 16:1–2)

Paul calls Phoebe "our sister"—more communal, familial language. He describes her as a "servant," which says something of her posture as an influencer. She has been a *patron*, Paul says. The word *patron* used here is a translation of προστάτις (*prostatis*), which can also have the connotation of *benefactor* or simply a helpful friend. Clearly, Phoebe had been a very influential figure in the port village of Cenchreae and probably nearby Corinth as well. In this commendation, Paul is requesting help for Phoebe, a woman who has made it her business to help others and may not be inclined to ask for assistance. It is notable that a woman would have this level of influence in a world that was so patriarchal.

Let's look at another commendation:

> Now I urge you, brothers—you know that the **household of Stephanas** were the <u>first converts in Achaia</u>, and that they have <u>devoted</u> themselves to the

service of the saints—be subject to such as these, and
to every fellow worker and laborer. I rejoice at the
coming of **Stephanas** and **Fortunatus** and **Achaicus**, because they have made up for your absence,
for they refreshed my spirit as well as yours. Give
recognition to such people. (1 Cor. 16:15–18)

Apparently Stephanas and his household were the first
to accept Christ in the southern part of Greece, known as
Achaia. These people were devoted servants, according to
Paul. He calls them "fellow workers," i.e., valued team members. Paul is encouraging his Corinthian readers to be subject
to people like them. He is trying to get the Corinthians to
understand the mutual submission that is crucial for Christian community. The three named individuals—Stephanas,
Fortunatus, and Achaicus—have "refreshed" Paul's spirit.
They played a valuable and often overlooked role: refreshing
and encouraging an exhausted onstage leader like Paul.

RELATIONSHIPS IN GREETINGS

Aristarchus my fellow prisoner greets you, and
Mark the cousin of Barnabas (concerning whom
you have received instructions—if he comes to you,
welcome him), and **Jesus who is called Justus**.
These are the only men of the circumcision among
my fellow workers for the kingdom of God, and they
have been a comfort to me. **Epaphras**, who is one
of you, a servant of Christ Jesus, greets you, always
struggling on your behalf in his prayers, that you

may stand mature and fully assured in all the will of God. For I bear him witness that <u>he has worked hard</u> for you and for those in Laodicea and in Hierapolis. **Luke** <u>the beloved physician</u> greets you, as does **Demas**. Give my greetings to **the brothers at Laodicea**, and to **Nympha** and the **church in her house**. And when this letter has been read among you, have it also read in the **church of the Laodiceans**; and see that you also read the letter from Laodicea. And say to **Archippus**, "<u>See that you fulfill the ministry that you have received in the Lord.</u>" (Col. 4:10–17)

In this text, Paul names a number of valuable people in his circle. Aristarchus was with Paul in prison. He commends Mark to the Colossians, the same man with whom he once had a falling out, and who went on to write the gospel of Mark. Paul also makes sure his readers know that Mark is related to Barnabas, another highly regarded leader. Paul notes that Justus, Mark, and Aristarchus are all Jewish ("men of the circumcision"), and have been not only "fellow workers," but a "comfort" to him. Again, Paul is letting his readers know that he is not an island; he needs friends and coworkers who build him up.

Paul also highlights Epaphras, who, he notes, was from the same area as his readers. Epaphras, a "servant," has been praying fervently for the Colossian readers, and Paul wanted them to know it. Paul also mentions that Luke—"the beloved physician"—is with him, and also someone named Demas.

Next, Paul said hello to a few groups of people who lived in the nearby city of Laodicea, most notably the church that meets in the house of a woman named Nympha. Here we catch another glimpse of an influential woman in the first-century church. Paul closes this section with an encouraging message to Archippus. It seems that Paul assumed Archippus would know what he was referring to.

We are going to look at one more text, and it's the longest. Resist the temptation to skim this, because it's a treasure trove of insight into Paul's team and his temperament as a leader.

> Greet **Prisca** and **Aquila**, my <u>fellow workers</u> in Christ Jesus, who <u>risked their necks</u> for my life, to whom not only I give thanks but all the churches of the Gentiles give thanks as well. Greet also **the church in their house**. Greet my beloved **Epaenetus**, who was the <u>first convert to Christ in Asia</u>. Greet **Mary**, who has <u>worked hard for you</u>. Greet **Andronicus and Junia**, my <u>kinsmen and my fellow prisoners</u>. They are well known to the apostles, and they were <u>in Christ before me</u>. Greet **Ampliatus**, my <u>beloved</u> in the Lord. Greet **Urbanus**, our <u>fellow worker</u> in Christ, and my <u>beloved</u> **Stachys**. Greet **Apelles**, who is <u>approved in Christ</u>. Greet those who belong to the **family of Aristobulus**. Greet <u>my kinsman</u> **Herodion**. Greet those in the Lord who belong to the **family of Narcissus**. Greet those <u>workers in the Lord</u>, **Tryphaena** and **Tryphosa**. Greet the beloved **Persis**, who has <u>worked hard in the Lord</u>. Greet **Rufus**, <u>chosen</u> in the Lord; also **his mother**, who has been a <u>mother to me as well</u>. Greet **Asyncritus, Phlegon, Hermes, Patrobas, Hermas,** and **the**

brothers who are with them. Greet **Philologus, Julia, Nereus** and **his sister,** and **Olympas,** and **all the saints who are with them** . . . The grace of our Lord Jesus Christ be with you. **Timothy**, my <u>fellow worker</u>, greets you; so do **Lucius** and **Jason** and **Sosipater**, my <u>kinsmen</u>. I **Tertius**, <u>who wrote this letter</u>, greet you in the Lord. **Gaius**, who is <u>host to me and to the whole church</u>, greets you. **Erastus**, the <u>city treasurer</u>, and <u>our brother</u> **Quartus**, greet you. (Rom. 16:3–15, 20–23)

This text shows the attention to detail and forethought that Paul put into these portions of his letters. He is making the most of a letter that would take a lot of time and effort to deliver. Paul seems to have racked his brain to think of anyone on the receiving end of the letter whom he wanted to greet, and also anyone with him who might want to say hello. It's remarkable the amount of energy Paul exerted to finish the highly theological letter to the Romans on such a social note.

I won't go through every person mentioned, but I will highlight some of the more notable comments. Overall, we see some of the same tendencies in this section as we've seen in the others: calling attention to fellow workers and noting their sacrifices (e.g., that Prisca and Aquila risked their necks for Paul's life). He greets house churches and households, and notes when someone was the first convert in a particular area. Paul points it out when someone is a prisoner, and highlights their family relations. In a particularly fascinating remark, Paul comments that his relatives Andronicus and Junia were

Christians before he was and were well known to the apostles. Paul also mentions that Rufus's mother has been a mother to him, once again noting when someone had cared for him. Paul did not hesitate to admit that he, too, needed care.

Paul wraps up by offering greetings to the Roman recipients from people with him. Tertius, who wrote down the letter for Paul, also greets the readers. It is probable that Paul dictated many of his letters to a trained scribe like Tertius, known as an amanuensis.[3] Paul also acknowledges who is hosting him (Gaius), and says hello from the city treasurer of Corinth, Erastus.

WHAT THIS MEANS FOR US TODAY

What are we to make of all this data? How does this change our view of Paul and his team? What conclusions can we draw for ourselves as we seek to honor God in the way that we lead and influence others?

In these sections, we see a picture of Paul stewarding relationships—maintaining connections with people he knew and also nurturing new relationships. It is clear that Paul genuinely cared for these people, but he also put forth a lot of energy to see these relationships flourish over the long haul. It's almost as if Paul viewed the relationships in his ministry as not only personal blessings to him, but also tangible resources that he was entrusted to steward. I like to think of Paul as something like an ancient switchboard operator, continually making connections and encouraging relational growth among his team.

Taking all the data together from the texts we looked at in this chapter, Paul seems to have been very deliberate about doing a handful of things in these sections of his letters:

- He provided general updates about his ministry.
- He gave spiritual encouragement with a tone of friendship.
- He deflected attention from himself and elevated others.[4]
- He highlighted the character and efforts of others.
- He fostered warm camaraderie by using affectionate, familial language.
- He encouraged mutual submission and reciprocal support among the believers.
- He candidly admitted his own need for encouragement and thanked those who had provided him that sort of refreshment.

How can we apply these strategies in our own context? Communication is a natural part of influence. We cannot choose whether we are influencers and whether we are communicators. The only choice we have is what *kind* of influencer we will be and what shape our communication will take.

Taking our cue from Paul and his team, we should keep people in the loop with how we're doing personally, spiritually, and professionally. We should look for opportunities to spiritually encourage others in the context of genuine friendships. We should take every chance to deflect attention from ourselves and highlight the achievements and character of others. We should find ways to foster warm camaraderie among those we lead or influence. We should sacrifice for others and encourage others to make sacrifices when they see needs. Perhaps most significantly, we should openly admit our own need for support and candidly ask others for help—and publicly thank them when they give it.

When we communicate about the kinds of things that Paul did, we make it clear that we don't think we are more special or valuable than the people we lead, and we develop a rapport of friendship, care, and openness. That sort of posture generates the kind of warm solidarity that Paul and his team had, and that we desperately need in the church today.

What does this look like in the twenty-first century? It can and should take a variety of forms based on the unique personality of the influencer. Send group texts in which you celebrate what God has done, and thank people for what they've done for the kingdom. Hit reply all to emails and brag about someone who did something remarkable. View yourself as a journalist among your team—taking pictures and gathering stories. Then tell those stories in church services, on blogs, on social media, and in newsletters. Shine a light on people who would never shine a light on themselves. Relate to people as a friend and equal. Remember their names. Listen to them. Ask them questions about their life over lunch, with no other agenda. Find ways to authentically thank them for their ministry and for what they personally mean to you. If you know two people who would be an encouragement or help to each other, get them talking. Make those connections like Paul did.

There are so many ways this can play out. When you're dealing with relationships, it's always more of an art than a science. But take the time to absorb these portions of Paul's letters and let his temperament and language take root in your heart. Ask God to make you the same kind of influencer and to show you how to cultivate that warm camaraderie that Paul and his team shared.

QUESTIONS FOR DISCUSSION/REFLECTION

- What stood out to you about this chapter?
- Why are relationships so important for influencers?
- What are the main reasons we tend to neglect relationships?
- How can you better steward the relationships in your circle of influence?
- How have you been led well by others? What is one practice you've seen in action that fostered the camaraderie that Paul experienced with his team?
- What did you find most challenging about this chapter?
- What is one thing you can change this week based on what you learned in this chapter?
- Sample Prayer: God, help me to view the relationships in my life as something I am supposed to steward—a resource that You have entrusted to me. Show me the ways in which I can build up Your church by fostering friendship and community, like Paul did. Help me to honor You in the way that I relate to others and in the way that I help others relate to each other. May the relationships in Your church bring You glory! Amen.

CHAPTER NINE

Relentless about Reconciliation

Restoring Relationships Even When It Hurts

As you might have noticed, there have been several conflict-oriented chapters in this book so far, and here is one more. Conflicts take a variety of forms, and the successful navigation and resolution of conflicts is a fundamental task of any Christian influencer. Sometimes it's about not writing someone off after a heated disagreement (as we discussed in chapter 4). In some cases, it's about picking our battles in the first place (ch. 5). In other instances, it's about addressing broader systemic divisions in our communities (ch. 7). Sometimes, however, conflict resolution is about dealing with deep, personal hurts, in which resolution or reconciliation seems truly impossible. That is what this chapter is about.

Restoring broken relationships is hard. True restoration requires love and forgiveness to spring up out of the parched soil of profound hurt. This kind of reconciliation is only possible through the action of the Holy Spirit. If we're honest with ourselves, most of us are not that optimistic about reconciliation, especially when the wound is deep. So we just move on. Or we spiritualize the situation, chalking it up to God's will that the relationship is over. Or we vilify the one who has harmed us as a fundamentally toxic person, which is a rather efficient way for us to avoid any personal responsibility.

To make matters worse, we sometimes find ourselves looking to Scripture to find reasons why we *shouldn't* continue to work for reconciliation. We misappropriate Romans 12:18: "If possible, so far as it depends on you, live peaceably with all." We use Paul's words as permission to stop making efforts to secure peace with someone. We use this verse as an excuse to evade responsibility and wash our hands of deep divisions with someone who has hurt us. As with many maladies within the church, this is just one more variation of pride.

Both sides in painful conflicts find themselves believing that God is on their side, wishing that He would put the other party in its place—which is the very definition of malice. When we do pursue peace, sometimes it is for the wrong reasons. We don't actually want a restored relationship; we just don't want to be the one who *doesn't* follow Jesus' standards of forgiveness and peacemaking. In effect, we're acting like Pharisees. We want to be the spiritually mature one in the conflict. The one who handled everything biblically. The one who is on the high road. I have been offered this sort of pseudo-reconciliation, and I have offered it to others. I'm betting you have too. It is pride in yet another costume.

We must be different. Christians are meant to be *relentless* about reconciliation. Christ gave everything to secure reconciliation with us, and we are called to model that same sort of love to the world around us—even to our enemies.

I do not say this flippantly. It is exceedingly difficult to pursue peace with someone who has wounded you. I have been hurt by people close to me, and when that happens it is a daily pain that seems to last forever. There have been many moments when I didn't feel interested in reconciliation. But God deals with me when that attitude rears its head. He reminds me that He loves the person who hurt me, and that I have a responsibility to show grace toward them in the same way He has given me His grace. God has taught me in a variety of ways that if I don't walk toward reconciliation, bitterness will fossilize in my heart—and stay there.

I have found that when I am obedient and take steps to reconcile, God begins to heal me through the process. Even if it doesn't turn out how I would have liked. Even if I don't receive the apology I was hoping for, God removes the bitterness from my heart and brings me to a place where I can pray for that person and hope for the restoration of the relationship. Over time the wounds scab over and turn to painless scars. God heals.

Paul experienced this type of pain within his ministry—pain coming not from outsiders or persecutors but from within the church. Pain coming from people he cared about and invested in. Paul was wounded by those he loved, and his response is instructive for us as we seek to be Christlike leaders and influencers. We get an unvarnished view of this raw situation in Paul's most personal and emotional letter: 2 Corinthians.

PAIN AND RECONCILIATION IN 2 CORINTHIANS

Paul had an ongoing correspondence with the church in Corinth in the mid-50s AD. We have two of those letters in our New Testament, but most scholars believe that there were many more, and that there were letters written between the two we call 1 and 2 Corinthians. We do not have any copies of letters sent from the church in Corinth to Paul, but Paul's words in 1 and 2 Corinthians make it clear that the church in Corinth was dealing with all sorts of internal and external threats to unity.

They also had a mixed relationship with Paul. In 1 Corinthians, Paul seems to be addressing factions within the church in Corinth over his leadership. Apparently some people in that congregation were disparaging Paul's leadership and pledging allegiance to other leaders whom they preferred. This is clear from what Paul wrote in 1 Corinthians 1:11–13:

> It has been reported to me by Chloe's people that there is quarreling among you, my brothers. What I mean is that each one of you says, "I follow Paul," or "I follow Apollos," or "I follow Cephas," or "I follow Christ." Is Christ divided? Was Paul crucified for you? Or were you baptized in the name of Paul?

Paul spends the remainder of 1 Corinthians addressing a variety of contentious issues within the church at Corinth, including sexual immorality, lawsuits, marriage, the place of spiritual gifts, and the misuse of the Lord's Supper. The Corinthians needed a lot of guidance.

At some point after Paul wrote 1 Corinthians, things went further south between him and the Corinthian Christians, as evidenced by what we read in 2 Corinthians. Paul writes 2 Corinthians as a pastor deeply concerned about the church at Corinth, and he candidly displays an array of emotions. Paul expresses anxiety, love, hurt, and joy. This is clear early in the letter:

> I made up my mind not to make another painful visit to you. For if I cause you pain, who is there to make me glad but the one whom I have pained? And I wrote as I did, so that when I came I might not suffer pain from those who should have made me rejoice, for I felt sure of all of you, that my joy would be the joy of you all. For I wrote to you out of much affliction and anguish of heart and with many tears, not to cause you pain but to let you know the abundant love that I have for you. (2 Cor. 2:1–4)

Paul evidently made a visit to Corinth that did not go well, and had subsequently written a tearful letter to express and affirm his love for the Corinthians. Reading 2 Corinthians is like walking into the middle of a painful family fight that has been going on for some time. Emotions are running high. At some points, Paul seems determined to defend himself and his status as an apostle (especially chapters 10–11). At other points, he sets himself aside for the greater purpose of reconciliation. Because we don't have all of the letters (and none sent from the Corinthians to Paul), there is a great deal of scholarly discussion about exactly what was going on here.

What is clear, however, is that Paul relied on his valued teammate Titus in this painful situation. Titus was Paul's envoy to the Corinthians during this challenging season. Titus was one of Paul's most trusted coworkers. He is mentioned by name thirteen times in the New Testament, though he is never mentioned in the book of Acts. He is primarily known to us through sporadic references in Paul's letters, and by the letter Paul sent to him that bears his name.

We know that Titus was Greek, and that he accompanied Paul and Barnabas in some of their early ministry travels (Gal. 2:1ff). Paul described Titus as his "true child in a common faith" (Titus 1:4). Paul typically uses this parental language when describing someone he led to Christ. Titus seems to have been a thick-skinned individual, because Paul deployed him into some especially difficult situations: the division with the church in Corinth, and establishing leadership for the new churches on the island of Crete (more on that in chapter 11).[1]

In the case of the rift with the church in Corinth, it's possible that Titus carried the tearful letter that Paul referred to in 2 Corinthians. Paul had traveled to Troas (on the west coast of Turkey) and was engaged in ministry there, but he felt he could not continue because of his preoccupation with the Corinthian situation. It seems that he was waiting to hear something from Titus: "When I came to Troas to preach the gospel of Christ, even though a door was opened for me in the Lord, my spirit was not at rest because I did not find my brother Titus there. So I took leave of them and went on to Macedonia" (2 Cor. 2:12–13).

Eventually Paul did connect with Titus and learn the Corinthians' response to his tearful letter. Paul is almost euphoric in describing his reaction:

> God, who comforts the downcast, comforted us by the coming of Titus, and not only by his coming but also by the comfort with which he was comforted by you, as he told us of your longing, your mourning, your zeal for me, so that I rejoiced still more. For even if I made you grieve with my letter, I do not regret it—though I did regret it, for I see that that letter grieved you, though only for a while. As it is, I rejoice, not because you were grieved, but because you were grieved into repenting. For you felt a godly grief, so that you suffered no loss through us.
>
> For godly grief produces a repentance that leads to salvation without regret, whereas worldly grief produces death. For see what earnestness this godly grief has produced in you, but also what eagerness to clear yourselves, what indignation, what fear, what longing, what zeal, what punishment! At every point you have proved yourselves innocent in the matter. So although I wrote to you, it was not for the sake of the one who did the wrong, nor for the sake of the one who suffered the wrong, but in order that your earnestness for us might be revealed to you in the sight of God. Therefore we are comforted.
>
> And besides our own comfort, we rejoiced still more at the joy of Titus, because his spirit has been refreshed by you all. For whatever boasts I made to him about you, I was not put to shame. But just

as everything we said to you was true, so also our boasting before Titus has proved true. And his affection for you is even greater, as he remembers the obedience of you all, how you received him with fear and trembling. I rejoice, because I have complete confidence in you. (2 Cor. 7:6–16)

This passage shows the emotional roller coaster that Paul had been on, and you can sense the palpable relief he felt when he found Titus and learned of the Corinthians' reaction to his letter. Paul seems to have been worried that he was too harsh in his previous letter. He had been agonizing over this situation, and when you think about how painfully slow travel and communication were in those days, it is clear that Paul had for some time been greatly burdened by and for the Corinthians.

By the end of the letter, Paul shifts back to a defensive posture. While the immediate crisis may have been averted, there are still deeper issues to be worked out with the Corinthians. There is still pain. There is still brokenness. At the end of the letter he writes:

Your restoration is what we pray for. For this reason I write these things while I am away from you, that when I come I may not have to be severe in my use of the authority that the Lord has given me for building up and not for tearing down. Finally, brothers, rejoice. Aim for restoration, comfort one another, agree with one another, live in peace; and the God of love and peace will be with you. (2 Cor. 13:9–11).

Paul's words in 2 Corinthians make it clear that he was relentless about reconciliation. He wasn't just open to it. He didn't just hope for it. He *worked* for it.

WHAT THIS MEANS FOR US TODAY

The unyielding pursuit of reconciliation is a hallmark of Christian influence, and Paul set a beautiful example for us in how he dealt with the Corinthians. He pursued reconciliation, and communicated explicitly to the Corinthians that reconciliation is what he was after. In the middle of this painful letter, he wrote this:

> If anyone is in Christ, he is a new creation. The old has passed away; behold, the new has come. All this is from God, who through Christ reconciled us to himself and gave us the ministry of reconciliation; that is, in Christ God was reconciling the world to himself, not counting their trespasses against them, and entrusting to us the message of reconciliation. Therefore, we are ambassadors for Christ, God making his appeal through us. We implore you on behalf of Christ, be reconciled to God. (2 Cor. 5:17–20)

For someone who has encountered Christ, reconciliation should be a top priority. The work of Christ on the cross was the definitive act of reconciliation between God and humanity. As a result, we Christians have been given the ministry of reconciliation, as Paul puts it. Because of Christ, our trespasses are no longer held against us, and we have the same ability and responsibility to forgive others. We are ambassadors for Christ—we represent Him—and the way we forgive and reconcile with others is a powerful indicator of what we think of ourselves and what we think of God. Paul is giving us the theological basis for relentlessly pursuing reconciliation with others. We do it as a reflection of what Christ did for us, and we do it because we are His ambassadors. The way we handle broken relationships represents Christ to a watching world.

It's no stretch to say that reconciliation is a key theme of 2 Corinthians. That idea is manifested throughout the letter, and Paul uses the Greek word for reconciliation, καταλλάσσω (*katallassō*), more in this letter than in any other place in his writings (Rom 5:10; 1 Cor. 7:11; 2 Cor. 5:18–20). That word has the connotation of trading something for something else, in this case exchanging "hostility for a friendly relationship."[2]

What does this mean for us? What do we take away from Paul's broken relationship with the Corinthians and how he and Titus worked for restoration? First, we have to embrace what Paul wrote in 2 Corinthians 5. We have to understand the lengths to which God went to reconcile with us. We have to allow that to burrow down into our hearts. If we do, we will be compelled to seek peace with others, because we understand how far God went to reconcile with us. We will no longer be comfortable allowing broken relationships to waste away.

Sometimes we are the Paul in a broken relationship. We feel hurt, perhaps even betrayed, and yet we still diligently pursue peace. We don't ever get to the place of being okay with division. Of course there are extreme exceptions, as in the case of abusive relationships, but that's not what we're talking about here. We're talking about relatively healthy relationships that turn sour and get buried under a mountain of pain. We've got to dig out and restore those relationships.

Sometimes we have to be the Titus in the situation. If we see people or groups at odds with each other, we need to view ourselves as brokers of reconciliation. We need to get people talking, and help them hear each other. When someone hurts us, that pain can create an invisible force field around us that prevents us from hearing what that person has to say. The force field either prevents us from listening at all, or, if something gets through, we hear a skewed version of what the person said.

We also don't articulate ourselves well when we've been hurt. In many cases of conflict, the person who initiates reconciliation expresses themselves clumsily, and the other person (who also wants reconciliation) hears a distorted version of what was said. That's where a Titus can be so helpful—someone who can make sure things are verbalized with clarity and heard accurately. Look for opportunities to be a Titus! You can foster reconciliation even if you're not a direct part of the conflict.

Unaddressed anger and malice is like flesh-eating bacteria, ruthlessly eating away at our hearts and replacing them with a heart of stone or cynicism. Remember, Satan is always looking to stoke division and fan it into an inferno. He is rooting against reconciliation because it is an especially powerful testament to who Christ is.

In his classic book *The Screwtape Letters,* C. S. Lewis imagines a series of letters sent from a veteran demon named Screwtape to his nephew Wormwood. Screwtape writes to advise the novice Wormwood on how to most effectively distract a man from knowing Christ and following Him with his whole heart. Screwtape refers to this man as Wormwood's "patient." In one of his letters, Screwtape gives this advice to his nephew:

> Do what you will, there is going to be some bene-volence, as well as some malice, in your patient's soul. The great thing is to direct the malice to his immediate neighbours whom he meets every day and to thrust his benevolence out to the remote circum-ference, to people he does not know. The malice thus becomes wholly real and the benevolence largely imaginary.[3]

Lewis's point is that it is hardest to show grace toward those in our lives, and easiest to show benevolence toward people we do not know—who live in faraway places. This is why many of us can so willingly spend energy and resources to support foreign missions or other humanitarian causes, while simul-taneously holding years-long grudges against close friends or family members. We are inexperienced with showing grace and seeking reconciliation when the hurt is deep and the re-lationship is close. Satan knows this, so he wants to keep our love toward others as theoretical and distant as possible. And he wants us to think that's enough.

Being relentless about reconciliation shows the world we are different. We Christians love our enemies. We view others as better than ourselves. We turn the other cheek. We treat people how we would want to be treated. We exchange hostility for friendship. We reconcile. Paul and Titus acted this out in their painful dilemma with the Corinthians, and we who follow Christ should ask the Holy Spirit to enable us to be the same type of influencers today.

QUESTIONS FOR DISCUSSION/REFLECTION

- What stood out to you about this chapter?
- Why is it so hard to reconcile with those who are close to us?
- Have you ever been on the receiving end of someone's effort to reconcile with you? How did you react?
- In what ways have you played the role of Titus in your life—helping to broker a difficult reconciliation?
- How does reconciliation uniquely illustrate the gospel?
- What did you find most challenging about this chapter?
- What is one thing you can change this week based on what you learned in this chapter?
- Sample Prayer: Heavenly Father, I want to be Your ambassador of reconciliation to the world around me. I understand that in order to do that, I must be willing to reconcile with those who have hurt me, or those whom I have hurt. I need Your help in this area. Sometimes I don't realize it when reconciliation needs to happen. Sometimes I balk when others try to reconcile with me. Please mature me in this area—give me an appetite for reconciliation. A desire to see relationships restored, even when it's painful. I trust You to guide me. Amen.

CHAPTER TEN

Trust in the Fog

Leading When You Seem to Be Losing

I 've heard it said that Christianity no longer has the home-field advantage in America. It's a poignant way to describe the shifting cultural landscape in the United States. In previous generations, there was some level of social expectation to at least uphold the *appearance* of being a Christian. In most parts of the country, that pressure no longer exists. As a result, Christians can no longer assume that the majority of people in their communities, neighborhoods, and workplaces share their beliefs or have basic familiarity with the Bible. This does not mean that there is necessarily hostility toward Christians, but there is an uphill climb to explain what we believe and why someone who doesn't believe it should take it seriously.

There are a number of precincts in our society in which it can seem like Christianity is "losing": social media, certain political contexts, and especially university campuses.

(Globally speaking, however, Christianity is still growing steadily.[1]) Our individual experiences can be discouraging when it feels like we're losing the battle to impact our communities for Christ. This affects our outlook and the choices we make as influencers.

How do we keep leading when there seems to be a growing swell of opposition? The title of this chapter is a little tongue-in-cheek, because I'm not a big fan of the winning/losing language that is so common to church leadership these days. It's too easy for that language to cultivate a climate of competition within and between congregations. But sometimes, when it comes to our engagement with broader society, it can feel like we're engaged in a losing battle.

Paul and his team certainly seemed to be losing in a number of situations. We will explore two of them in this chapter. In both scenarios, the gospel was going into a pagan environment for the first time, and Paul was trying to contextualize a Jewish savior for a Greco-Roman audience. In one instance there was a language barrier in play, and in the other there were vested commercial interests fighting against the message of Christ. At the time, Paul and his team seemed to be losing—at least judging by outward appearances. But they kept leading in the fog of discouragement and opposition, and God worked powerfully through them.

OPPOSITION IN LYSTRA

Lystra was a relatively small town in the region of Galatia (modern Turkey), and I love the account of Paul and Barnabas visiting there. The story is tucked away in the weeds of Acts, but it's one of my favorite episodes in Paul's ministry (Acts 14:8–20). It's almost comical how many challenges came at Paul and Barnabas. They walk into Lystra, and Paul heals a man who had been unable to walk since birth. That's a fairly dramatic miracle, and the locals responded immediately and passionately:

> Now at Lystra there was a man sitting who could not use his feet. He was crippled from birth and had never walked. He listened to Paul speaking. And Paul, looking intently at him and seeing that he had faith to be made well, said in a loud voice, "Stand upright on your feet." And he sprang up and began walking. And when the crowds saw what Paul had done, they lifted up their voices, saying in Lycaonian, "The gods have come down to us in the likeness of men!" Barnabas they called Zeus, and Paul, Hermes, because he was the chief speaker. (Acts 14:8–12)

There are a few key challenges going on here. Because no mention is made of a Jewish synagogue, there would have been no shared religious heritage with the residents of Lystra. Luke also mentions that the crowd responded to Paul's miracle by crying out in the Lycaonian language, a local dialect that Paul and Barnabas probably did not understand very well (if at all). Most of Paul's ministry was conducted in Greek, the common language of the Roman Empire.

In addition to the language barrier, there's this religious

confusion at work. The locals think that Paul and Barnabas are Zeus, the king of the Greek gods, and Hermes, Zeus's chief messenger. Luke even describes that the priest of Zeus in Lystra wanted to offer a sacrifice to Paul and Barnabas! It's safe to say they did not feel like they were winning at this moment.

It's unclear why exactly this confusion happened, but one possibility is a local legend about Zeus and Hermes having visited in the past. Apparently on the previous visit, the locals did not show them hospitality, and they were punished for it.[2] The people of Lystra may have been trying to avoid a similar fate this time.

In any case, Paul and Barnabas needed to stop the madness and help the people of Lystra understand their message about Jesus. They desperately needed to find some common ground. In the midst of the chaos, Paul spoke these words, hoping, I assume, that they would understand at least some of it:

> "Men, why are you doing these things? We also are men, of like nature with you, and we bring you good news, that you should turn from these vain things to a living God, who made the heaven and the earth and the sea and all that is in them. In past generations he allowed all the nations to walk in their own ways. Yet he did not leave himself without witness, for he did good by giving you rains from heaven and fruitful seasons, satisfying your hearts with food and gladness." (Acts 14:15–17)

Paul spoke about Christ in a way that the people of Lystra might understand. He could not talk about Jesus as he would with native Greek speakers or with Jews in the synagogues. He spoke in Lystra about God the Creator, a concept somewhat familiar to them. He also spoke about how God is the provider who gives us rains and crops to provide food. This, too, would have been a familiar concept to pagans. He adds at the end that God is the provider of gladness, a universal emotion and desire.

Did you notice what Paul did *not* say? He did not mention anything about Scripture. He did not tell any stories from the Old Testament. He did not even mention the name of Jesus Christ. It is a similar tactic he used with the Areopagus in Athens. Paul wanted to meet the people of Lystra on their terms and begin a conversation on some sort of common ground. He was adapting, in real time, to the challenges as they presented themselves.

But there were more waves of trouble coming, because Paul's passionate explanation of Christ wasn't getting through to them:

> Even with these words they scarcely restrained the people from offering sacrifice to them. But Jews came from Antioch and Iconium, and having persuaded the crowds, they stoned Paul and dragged him out of the city, supposing that he was dead. But when the disciples gathered about him, he rose up and entered the city, and on the next day he went on with Barnabas to Derbe. When they had preached the gospel to

that city and had made many disciples, they returned to Lystra and to Iconium and to Antioch, strengthening the souls of the disciples, encouraging them to continue in the faith, and saying that through many tribulations we must enter the kingdom of God. (Acts 14:18–22)

Paul did not win them over—at least not in that moment. Some opponents of the gospel had followed Paul to Lystra, and they were successful in winning over the crowds. In fact, Paul almost died because of this. They threw rocks at him until he was so badly injured that they thought he was dead. Paul did not seem to be winning.

But even after almost dying, Paul went back into the city. And then, after leaving and visiting some other cities, he came *back* through Lystra again at a later date. He did not give up on them. He knew they needed Christ and that God could do a powerful work there, even if it seemed from a human perspective that the gospel was losing.

One of the most long-lasting outcomes of Paul's difficult ministry in Lystra is that he found Timothy there, his closest friend and arguably his most important ministry partner (Acts 16:1).[3] When Paul wrote to Timothy many years later, he said this: "I am reminded of your sincere faith, a faith that dwelt first in your grandmother Lois and your mother Eunice and now, I am sure, dwells in you as well" (2 Tim. 1:5). An entire family tree—at least three generations including Timothy—was forever impacted by Paul's ministry in Lystra, which got off to a really rough start.

What would have happened if Paul had given up or interpreted the challenges he faced as a sign from God to move on? The same God who led Paul through the predicament at Lystra works in our lives every day. Who knows what outcome God has in store for us if we trust Him in the fog? Just because we face difficult seasons as leaders doesn't necessarily mean that we're doing something wrong. God wants to use our influence in situations that seem desperate or impossible to us.

OPPOSITION IN EPHESUS

Compared to most cities where Paul and his team operated, Ephesus was enormous. It dwarfed rustic towns like Lystra in both size and influence. Ephesus was a true metropolis—one of the largest cities in the Roman Empire, boasting a population somewhere north of two hundred thousand people. Ephesus was located on the western coast of modern Turkey, and it was one of the most famous and influential cities of the time.

Ephesus was fiercely devoted to the goddess Artemis. The Ephesians built a temple for her that was so large it was considered to be one of the seven wonders of the ancient world. With the exception of the pyramids in Egypt, the Temple of Artemis at Ephesus was quite possibly the largest enclosed structure in the world at that time. The Greeks worshiped Artemis as the virgin goddess of the hunt, which is why she is typically depicted with a bow and arrow. At Ephesus, however, Greek Artemis was blended with local mother goddesses from the environs of Ephesus. As a result, the Ephesians worshiped her primarily as a fertility goddess. Surviving sculptures of Ephesian Artemis depict her as a multi-breasted mother-goddess.

People would come from all over the Roman world to worship Artemis at Ephesus. It is no stretch to say that the Ephesians were fanatical about Artemis and felt great pride that their city was the keeper of her temple.[4] It was into this environment that Paul brought the message of Christ. It's not hard to imagine that there would be resistance; Artemis had the clear home-field advantage.

When Paul arrived, he went to the Jewish community first—his *modus operandi*, as we have seen. He knew *they* wouldn't be loyal to Artemis. According to the book of Acts, Paul spent three months teaching the Jews about Christ until they asked him to move on. Paul then spent the next two years teaching daily in the lecture hall of Tyrannus, a private venue where he was allowed to share the message of Christ (Acts 19:8ff). Between his time in the Jewish synagogues and his stint in the lecture hall, Paul had been sharing Christ with Ephesus for about twenty-seven months. Luke tells us in the book of Acts that many people in the region of Ephesus—both Jews and Gentiles—heard the message of Christ through the ministry of Paul and his team. Things seemed to be going well for a time, but then some of the Ephesians pushed back.

Luke describes the dramatic confrontation:

> About that time there arose no little disturbance concerning the Way. For a man named Demetrius, a silversmith, who made silver shrines of Artemis, brought no little business to the craftsmen. These

he gathered together, with the workmen in similar trades, and said, "Men, you know that from this business we have our wealth. And you see and hear that not only in Ephesus but in almost all of Asia this Paul has persuaded and turned away a great many people, saying that gods made with hands are not gods. And there is danger not only that this trade of ours may come into disrepute but also that the temple of the great goddess Artemis may be counted as nothing, and that she may even be deposed from her magnificence, she whom all Asia and the world worship." When they heard this they were enraged and were crying out, "Great is Artemis of the Ephesians!" So the city was filled with the confusion, and they rushed together into the theater, dragging with them Gaius and Aristarchus, Macedonians who were Paul's companions in travel. But when Paul wished to go in among the crowd, the disciples would not let him. (Acts 19:23–30)

The grievance of the craftsmen was twofold: (1) The message of Christ was hurting them financially, and (2) The gospel was disrespecting Artemis and the greatness of Ephesus. In their anger, the craftsmen created a furor that generated a large-scale riot in the theater. *Stadium* might be a more descriptive term, because the colossal Ephesian theater could seat around twenty-five thousand spectators. It still stands today.

THEATER AT EPHESUS. PHOTO BY RYAN LOKKESMOE.

Luke tells us that the crowd in the theater shouted, "Great is Artemis of the Ephesians!" in unison for two hours before the city clerk showed up to calm them down and warn them about the consequences of rioting (Acts 19:35–41).

WHAT THIS MEANS FOR US TODAY

What lessons can we learn from Paul's ministry in Lystra and Ephesus? First, we need to be persistent when sharing Christ with those around us. After Paul was driven out of Lystra—and nearly killed—he went back. He eventually returned a third time. When he arrived in the great metropolis of Ephesus, he went to the Jewish community first but was eventually asked to leave. Even then, he did not interpret the rejection as evidence of God not wanting him to minister to Ephesus. Paul knew that the city was enslaved to the worship of Artemis, and he could not walk away. So he adapted and found another venue: the lecture hall of Tyrannus. God used that space as a platform for Paul to speak the truth for another two years. Imagine what would have happened if he didn't return to Lystra, and if he had just given up when the Jews in Ephesus asked him to leave their synagogues.

The ministry of Paul's team in Ephesus was so fruitful, in fact, that it actually made an impact on the sales of Artemis shrines. That's why the craftsmen were so upset; too many people were becoming Christians. They were worried that they would be out of a job. The riot in Acts 19 was a result of the steady, adaptive ministry of Paul and his team in that city for the previous two years. I imagine there were many moments leading up to (and even during) the riot when it seemed like the gospel was losing.

We as influencers for Christ have to be persistent like Paul and his team. We cannot forget that we are surrounded by people who desperately need Jesus and have given their allegiance to things that will one day be exposed as meaningless. We have to help them see the truth, even if Christianity as a whole seems to be losing ground in the culture.

The challenge is that there are Temples of Artemis in our world today, but they're invisible—temples of desires, thought patterns, attitudes, and behaviors. For the Ephesians, the god commanding their allegiance was made of marble. In that sense, they had it easier, because they could see the god they worshiped instead of Christ.

The idols that draw our allegiance away from God today are often invisible, though every bit as powerful and intoxicating. The invisible temples in our lives demand our allegiance and divide our devotion to Christ. For people who don't know Jesus, they don't even realize they're worshiping at invisible temples.

Thus, another thing we can learn from Paul is that we need to expose today's temples—like the temples of materialism, professional success, political perspective, reputation, and physical appearance. Sometimes the temples are even good gifts that we treasure too highly, like the temples of family, patriotism, or even the church as an institution, because even that can calcify and become a barrier to Christ in our hearts.

We must pray that God uses us to bring light into the dark places, as He did through Paul and his team in places like Lystra and Ephesus. In Lystra, Paul was nearly beaten to death. In Ephesus, a riot was started that could have resulted in significant death and destruction. But Paul and his team relied on God and stayed the course because they knew one fundamental fact that we all need to grasp: even people who *oppose* Jesus need Him.

When Paul wrote his letter to the Ephesians, he was writing to the Christians in Ephesus about a decade after the incident in the theater. It's possible that some members of the Ephesian church were among those shouting years earlier, "Great is Artemis of the Ephesians!" It's safe to say most of the Ephesian Christians had worshiped Artemis at some point in their past. To those people, Paul wrote these stirring words in Ephesians 2:1–5:

> As for you, you were dead in your transgressions and sins, in which you used to live when you followed the ways of this world and of the ruler of the kingdom of the air, the spirit who is now at work in those who

are disobedient. All of us also lived among them at one time, gratifying the cravings of our flesh and following its desires and thoughts. Like the rest, we were by nature deserving of wrath. But because of his great love for us, God, who is rich in mercy, made us alive with Christ even when we were dead in transgressions—it is by grace you have been saved. (NIV)

As we seek to influence those around us with the life-changing message of Christ, we have to remember that God does incredible works through people like you and me in situations that might seem impossible to us. The love of Christ expressed through the church can change hearts, lives, and the world. Timothy's family tree was changed by God's work in Lystra. Many Ephesians placed their faith in Christ—residents of a city that literally shouted the greatness of another god. If we make ourselves available to God, He will do through us the work that only He can do. We just have to trust Him.

QUESTIONS FOR DISCUSSION/REFLECTION

- What stood out to you about this chapter as a whole?
- What did you notice about the Lystra episode? (Acts 14:8–20)
- What did you observe about the riot in the Ephesian theater? (Acts 19:23–41)
- How are the two episodes similar? How are they different?

- What Temples of Artemis do you see in our culture? In your life?
- What did you find most challenging about this chapter?
- What is one thing you can change this week based on what you learned in this chapter?
- Sample Prayer: God, help me to see the temples in our culture. Help me to see the temples in my life—places where I might be worshiping someone or something other than You. Holy Spirit, guide me. Give me strength. Give me the persistence of Paul's team. Help me to forge ahead with sharing the gospel, even if the world around me doesn't seem very interested. Remind me that their apparent lack of interest has no bearing on how much they need You. Create in me a compassionate heart for those who reject You. Give me courage to speak the truth in love to my sphere of influence. I trust You. Amen.

CHAPTER ELEVEN

Fade to the Background

*Admitting You're Replaceable
and Grooming Your Replacements*

When I was in junior high, I ran track as a part of the sprint team. I enjoyed the individual events, but the relays were the most exciting because they were a team effort and they involved the surprisingly difficult task of passing the baton. If you've ever watched the sprint relays in the Olympics, you've seen that before a handoff is made, the next runner begins running. They have to achieve a certain speed before the previous runner arrives, so that they can take the baton in stride and start their leg of the race with minimal disruption. Even in elite levels of competition, some sprinters still drop the baton. I dropped it plenty of times back when I ran track.

The handoff of the baton is a powerful metaphor for leadership in any context, but certainly within the church.

At some point, whatever influence we have will be handed off to someone else. Someone will take over for us in whatever leadership role we currently occupy. If there is no one waiting for the baton, we risk squandering our influence. If there is someone waiting but they do not begin running before we arrive, then they are not adequately prepared for the race they're about to run. We have to make sure there are people waiting to run the next leg of the race, and we have to make sure they're running before we hand them the baton. We have to get them up to speed. It's also critical that we're carrying a baton in the first place—we have to grasp the fact that we will be replaced.

What would your world look like without you? Can you even imagine it? It's not natural to think about replacing ourselves. To do that, we must have the realism to acknowledge that we're mortal, the maturity to admit we're replaceable, and the foresight to find and prepare successors to take our place.

Think of Jesus' disciples. They were persecuted for their faith, and many of them died as martyrs. At the time, I imagine they seemed fairly irreplaceable to the rest of the church. *What will we do when Peter is gone? How will we manage without Paul?* I'm sure many first-century Christians thought about questions like that. But God in His sovereignty allowed the leadership of His church to pass safely into the hands of other capable leaders.[1]

The next generation of Christian influencers advanced the gospel in their communities, and then passed the baton on to someone else. Christian leaders have been replaced for centuries, and the church has forged ahead under their guidance. Christianity has passed political boundaries, language barriers, oceans and mountains; it has navigated all sorts of schisms, social persecution, and gross misrepresentations.

Here we are as Christian influencers today, inheriting the two-thousand-year-old legacy of leaders leading and being replaced. This is the simple fact you must acknowledge if you are going to step into this grand tradition: you are replaceable. So am I. We will be replaced someday, so we need to begin thinking proactively about the kind of person who might replace us. How can we set them up for success? How can we share our wisdom and experience with them so they have a better running start in leadership than we did?

So often we hoard our talents, in many cases unconsciously. In other cases, we keep our talents and insights to ourselves because we want to be unique or corner the market on a particular style of influence. That sort of thinking is pride in yet another disguise, and if we allow ourselves to think in those terms, we dishonor God (who gave us our gifts and talents) and we shortchange the next generation of leaders.

There are people in our spheres of influence in whom we should be investing. God wants us to share our wisdom, insights, experiences, and strategies with them. It could be your kids, a coworker, a friend, or a student. God might want you to develop them over a period of many years, or in a shorter concentrated season of training right now. Will you rise to the occasion?

Paul did this. If there was anyone in the first century who would have seemed truly irreplaceable to his team, it was him. But Paul didn't view himself that way. He cultivated a leadership legacy that echoed far beyond his lifetime.

It is fair to say that Paul didn't have much of a choice but to groom his replacements, considering how young and scattered the church was. He couldn't be everywhere at once, so he needed to develop trustworthy leaders to serve in his absence. This was especially true once he was imprisoned and facing the specter of his execution. In that sense, Paul was just doing what was necessary. He didn't have the luxury of keeping his leadership skills to himself. Most of us don't feel that same urgency in the church today because (at least in America) it can feel like the church is firmly established and that there are plenty of leaders to go around.

Unfortunately, that is not the case. According to the 2017 *State of Pastors* report published by the Barna Group and Pepperdine University, only 1 in 7 senior pastors in America is under the age of 40, and the average age of senior pastors is about a decade older than it was 25 years ago.[2] It seems that the church in America is struggling to find ways of passing the baton on to the next generation. We need to get more comfortable with loosening our grip and sharing the leadership responsibilities.

PREPARING FOR THE LOSS OF LEADERS

Paul made it a habit to identify young leaders with potential and invest in them over time. Throughout his ministry career there were nagging challenges that he addressed on many occasions—for example, false teaching and various forms of disunity among the congregations. As we have seen, Paul relied on key members of his team to help him negotiate these challenges. But once it got into the early mid-60s AD, the temperature of persecution began to rise as the public view toward Christianity changed from general suspicion to outright hostility. As a result, a new generation of Christian leaders was desperately needed—and fast.

The most infamous example of this persecution was Emperor Nero's actions in 64 AD, which led to the martyrdom of Peter, Paul, and a number of other early Christian leaders. A great fire had swept through Rome, and Nero scapegoated the small Christian community. According to the famed first-century Roman historian Tacitus, only four of Rome's fourteen districts emerged unscathed from the fire.[3] Tacitus describes how Nero arrested Christians, forced them to identify other Christians, and then made public spectacles of their executions. Nero lit his gardens with burning Christians, had others torn to pieces by animals for entertainment in the Circus, and crucified many.[4] This was perhaps the most extreme manifestation of persecution, but it would not be the last.

In the early second century, a Roman governor named Pliny wrote to Emperor Trajan to discuss how to handle the growing influence of the Christian community. He asked for Trajan's advice about how to punish the Christians. Should they be disciplined based on their actions, or is it a crime simply to *be* a Christian? In seeking his superior's advice, Pliny describes how he has dealt with suspected Christians:

> I have asked them in person if they are Christians, and if they admit it, I repeat the question a second and third time, with a warning of the punishment awaiting them. If they persist, I order them to be led away for execution; for, whatever the nature of their

admission, I am convinced that their stubbornness and unshakeable obstinacy ought not to go unpunished . . . I considered that I should dismiss any who denied that they were or ever had been Christians when they had repeated after me the formula of invocation to the gods and had made offerings of wine and incense to your statue . . . and furthermore had reviled the name of Christ: none of which things, I understand, any genuine Christian can be induced to do.[5]

For those of us who live in countries that protect our freedom to worship, hearing of a government-sponsored campaign of persecution against Christians seems unimaginable. But, we must not forget that this sort of violent persecution still occurs today in repressive regimes around the world. We also cannot fail to learn the lesson of the first century: the church had enough depth of prepared leadership that it could weather the storms of persecution and survive the loss of seemingly indispensable leaders.

We see evidence of Paul's deliberate investment in future leaders in hints throughout his letters. As we have seen, Paul was continually mentioning fellow workers and others who had been in the trenches with him. That's part of leadership development—just doing ministry alongside others who can see you in action and be inspired to follow in your footsteps.

But Paul seems to have also taken a special interest in a handful of leaders and invested in them on a deeper level, the most notable being Timothy and Titus. We know the kind of personal investment Paul made because of the letters he wrote to them that we have in our New Testament.

First and 2 Timothy and Titus have historically been referred to as the Pastoral Epistles because Paul sent them to men functioning in a pastoral capacity.

These three letters have a different purpose and feel to them than Paul's other letters. In the first place, they are written to individuals instead of groups of Christians. Second, they are written to men who are close to Paul and are in ministry leadership. When we read the Pastoral Epistles, we are overhearing a conversation between Christian leaders who have been working together for many years.

As Paul's ministry was drawing to a close, he entrusted these men with huge amounts of responsibility and counseled them from afar. They were now on the front lines, and Paul was observing and supporting them from a distance. How did Paul fade to the background and hand over responsibility to Timothy and Titus?

PREPARING TITUS

At the beginning of his letter to Titus, Paul writes, "To Titus, my true child in a common faith: Grace and peace from God the Father and Christ Jesus our Savior. This is why I left you in Crete, so that you might put what remained into order, and appoint elders in every town as I directed you" (Titus 1:4–5).

Paul was giving responsibility for the entire island of Crete to Titus. This was a big leadership role, because Crete is by far the largest of the Greek isles (over 150 miles long). Titus was tasked with raising up Christian leaders among the many towns on the island. Paul admits in his charge that there are things that need to be put in order. He goes on to explain the kind of character traits Titus should be looking for in the leaders he will appoint (Titus 1:6–9). Paul uses two terms for leadership in this text, seemingly interchangeably: πρεσβύτερος (*presbyteros*) and ἐπίσκοπος (*episkopos*). The former has to do with age, and is generally translated as "elder." The latter has more to do with function, literally meaning "overseer" (though sometimes translated rather anachronistically as "bishop").

There would be no shortage of challenges on the island of Crete. Paul gives us a snapshot of the uphill climb that he had delegated to Titus:

> There are many who are insubordinate, empty talkers and deceivers, especially those of the circumcision party. They must be silenced, since they are upsetting whole families by teaching for shameful gain what they ought not to teach. One of the Cretans, a prophet of their own, said, "Cretans are always liars, evil beasts, lazy gluttons." This testimony is true. Therefore rebuke them sharply, that they may be sound in the faith. (Titus 1:10–13)

Some of the issues with the Cretan churches were along the lines of the kinds of challenges Paul had seen in other contexts: quarrelsome members, false teaching, and those advocating for adherence to the Jewish law. Paul seems to indicate, however, that these issues were amplified by a culture in Crete that was especially challenging. Combined with the sheer size of the island, Titus had his work cut out for him.

Because Paul is speaking to a trusted friend in this letter, he does not sugarcoat anything. He just launches into the pragmatic aspects of leadership that he wants Titus to grasp. That said, at two points in the letter Paul does pause his practical advice to remind Titus of the *reason* why solid Christian leadership is so important and why people should behave in certain ways: the gospel. For Paul, everything comes back to the gospel of Christ. It is the foundation of every aspect of their shared ministry. For example, after listing a number of behaviors and attitudes that Titus should seek to cultivate among the Cretan Christians, he offers this for the reason:

> For the grace of God has appeared, bringing salvation for all people, training us to renounce ungodliness and worldly passions, and to live self-controlled, upright, and godly lives in the present age, waiting for our blessed hope, the appearing of the glory of our great God and Savior Jesus Christ, who gave himself for us to redeem us from all lawlessness and to purify for himself a people for his own possession who are zealous for good works. Declare these things; exhort and rebuke with all authority. Let no one disregard you. (Titus 2:11–15)

Because of God's grace, and because of the hope that we have in Christ, we should live a certain way and insist on proper doctrine. Our lives are a response to what Christ has already done for us. But in case Titus (or any future reader) thinks to put too much weight on their own shoulders, Paul notes in verse 12 that God's grace trains us to renounce the ways of the world.

Paul continues a few verses later in chapter 3, expanding on the same theme:

> ... when the goodness and loving kindness of God our Savior appeared, he saved us, not because of works done by us in righteousness, but according to his own mercy, by the washing of regeneration and renewal of the Holy Spirit, whom he poured out on us richly through Jesus Christ our Savior, so that being justified by his grace we might become heirs according to the hope of eternal life. The saying is trustworthy, and I want you to insist on these things, so that those who have believed in God may be careful to devote themselves to good works. These things are excellent and profitable for people. (Titus 3:4–8)

We are saved not by our moral strivings, but because of God's mercy and the renewal of the Holy Spirit. Paul is contextualizing leadership and Christian ethics for Titus. His leadership should be based on a firm understanding of the gospel of grace—it should drive his decisions as he leads the leaders of Crete. Titus should likewise work to contextualize Christian behavior for the Cretan Christians: they don't behave morally because they are trying to earn God's love or be good people. They behave like a Christian out of love for Christ, who gave Himself for them. Their life is a joyful, thankful response to the gospel. That's the key point Paul wanted to make sure Titus never forgot, and we must not forget it either as we influence our teams, kids, and anyone who looks to us as an example.

PREPARING TIMOTHY

In Paul's letters to Timothy, we see the same level of responsibility given to Timothy, and a similar sort of encouragement. Paul begins 1 Timothy with these words:

> To Timothy, my true child in the faith: Grace, mercy, and peace from God the Father and Christ Jesus our Lord. As I urged you when I was going to Macedonia, remain at Ephesus so that you may charge certain persons not to teach any different doctrine, nor to devote themselves to myths and endless genealogies, which promote speculations rather than the stewardship from God that is by faith. (1 Tim. 1:2–4)

It seems that Paul had entrusted Timothy with the ministry to Ephesus—an incredibly large and influential city, as we have seen. Implied in this charge is the fact that Paul has *already taught* Timothy the correct doctrine of Christ, which puts him in the position to teach the Ephesians the truth.

Toward the end of the letter, Paul gives Timothy a clear explanation as to *why* they work so hard to lead and influence the church:

> For to this end we toil and strive, because we have our hope set on the living God, who is the Savior of all people, especially of those who believe. Command and teach these things. Let no one despise you for your youth, but set the believers an example in speech, in conduct, in love, in faith, in purity. Until I

come, devote yourself to the public reading of Scripture, to exhortation, to teaching. (1 Tim. 4:10–13)

As in his letter to Titus, Paul is explaining that the reason we live a certain way as Christians is because of the hope we have in Christ our Savior. Everything always goes back to the gospel.

In 2 Timothy, as Paul is facing his impending execution, he gives this final charge of ministry to his longtime friend and ministry partner. Here we clearly see Paul handing off the baton to Timothy:

> I charge you in the presence of God and of Christ Jesus, who is to judge the living and the dead, and by his appearing and his kingdom: preach the word; be ready in season and out of season; reprove, rebuke, and exhort, with complete patience and teaching. For the time is coming when people will not endure sound teaching, but having itching ears they will accumulate for themselves teachers to suit their own passions, and will turn away from listening to the truth and wander off into myths. As for you, always be sober-minded, endure suffering, do the work of an evangelist, fulfill your ministry. For I am already being poured out as a drink offering, and the time of my departure has come. I have fought the good fight, I have finished the race, I have kept the faith. Henceforth there is laid up for me the crown of righteousness, which the Lord, the righteous judge, will award to me on that day, and not only to me but

also to all who have loved his appearing. Do your
best to come to me soon. (2 Tim. 4:1–9)

Paul knew that the end was near for him and most of the
first-generation Christian leaders, and he took seriously his
responsibility to prepare the church for the challenges ahead.
Paul led until the very end, but he did not hold on to control
or view himself as irreplaceable. He knew he was going to be
replaced, and acted accordingly.

Paul left behind a group of people who knew and loved
him, and they carried on his legacy. I imagine there were men
and women scattered around the Mediterranean world who
knew Paul so well that they could imagine how he would
handle the situations they were facing. *What would Paul do?*
I'm sure that question was asked in many congregations.

We see a glimpse of this next generation leadership in one
of the earliest Christian writings outside of the New Testament, a letter known as 1 Clement. Clement was a key leader
in the Roman church after the death of the apostles. The
letter was sent from the Roman Christians to the church in
Corinth, after hearing that there were damaging divisions and
painful disunity among the Corinthian Christians. Clement
wrote his letter to foster peace and unity in Corinth, advising
the Corinthians to do what Paul had previously counseled
them to do.[6] He writes,

Take up the epistle of the blessed Paul the apostle.
What did he first write to you in the beginning of
the gospel? Truly he wrote to you in the Spirit about
himself and Cephas and Apollos, because even then

you had split into factions . . . It is disgraceful, dear friends, yes, utterly disgraceful and unworthy of your conduct in Christ, that it should be reported that the well-established and ancient Church of the Corinthians, because of one or two persons, is rebelling against its presbyters. (1 Clement 47:1–6)[7]

In this text we sense that the next generation of Christians has assumed leadership of the church, and they are looking to the words of Paul—their forerunner—as the basis for how they now view leadership and Christian community. Their ability to lead well was due to the fact that the first generation of Christian leadership raised them up for difficult moments such as this.

WHAT THIS MEANS FOR US TODAY

We need to accept that God has us placed in our roles as influencers for a season. It might be a short season; it could be a lifelong endeavor. Regardless of what the role is— parent, teacher, pastor, boss, coach, or some other form of influence—it will not last forever. If we view ourselves as irreplaceable, we do a disservice to our ministries and those we influence, and we set the stage for future hardship that will fall into the laps of our successors.

If you're a parent, what worldview have you passed to your children? When you think about your own influence and leadership abilities, which you've acquired over a lifetime of education and experience, how well do you feel you have handed those skills and values off to your children? When they leave your home and go to college or enter the workforce, what will be the complexion of their spiritual influence, and how have you helped to shape it?

If you serve in pastoral ministry, there's another (perhaps uncomfortable) aspect of this discussion that we have to deal with, and it has to do with our pride and willingness to hear God's voice. If we view ourselves as the permanent, indispensable fixture around which our ministries are based, we might stop listening to God and not even realize it. What if God calls us to replace ourselves and go lead elsewhere? What if He wants to deploy us elsewhere in His kingdom? Would we even be able to hear Him if He did?

Ask yourself this diagnostic question: *can you imagine leaving your current leadership post and serving somewhere else?* If you can't, then you might be gripping too tightly to your role. You might have plugged your ears to God's voice. He might be calling you to another season of ministry in a different place. You may have already served your purpose in your current context, and it's time to pass the reins on to someone else.

If God asked you to leave your job in a year, would you hear Him? Be honest. Ask yourself questions like this: *If I was gone tomorrow, what structures and people would I have left behind me who could pick up the baton and continue the race? Is this place too dependent on me?*

This is just food for thought. It may be the case that God has you where you are for a reason and that He intends to keep you there for decades. But, we have to hold our roles loosely, because God might be calling someone else to take our place—perhaps sooner than we expect.

To hold our positions loosely means a couple of things:

(1) We teach others how to do what we do, and (2) We continually seek the Lord's guidance about whether we're supposed to move on. It's difficult to do that. It's painful to leave ministries or leadership roles that we love. Paul experienced that kind of pain on a continual basis, as he would leave congregations and move on to other parts of the world where people needed to know Jesus. But what would his ministry have looked like if he had only shared Christ in Antioch? What if he had never ventured into Galatia? What if he had never gone to Ephesus? Or Philippi? Or Thessalonica? Or Athens? Or Corinth? What if he hadn't invested in leaders along the way and taken some along on the journey with him? How different the landscape of first-century Christianity would have been. We all owe Paul and his team a debt for holding their positions loosely and investing in the people and the places that were next.

QUESTIONS FOR DISCUSSION/REFLECTION

- What stood out to you about this chapter?
- In what ways have others invested in you? How has it shaped your life?
- Why do you think it is so challenging to find and prepare our successors?
- What did you notice about what Paul wrote to Titus and Timothy?
- Why is it so important that the church have a plan for leadership development?
- What did you find most challenging about this chapter?

- What is one thing you can change this week based on what you learned in this chapter?
- Sample Prayer: Dear Lord, help me to recognize that I am replaceable, and to honestly seek You about the nature of my influence. Show me where You want me to serve in Your kingdom, and help me to hold my current leadership roles loosely. Show me the people in my life You would like me to disciple. Help me to invest in the next generation of leaders, even as I struggle to lead well right now. Please show me any areas of pride that are lurking in my heart and may cripple my ability to hand off the baton. I trust You. Guide me, Lord. Amen.

Our Peculiar Posture

Three centuries after Paul wrote his letters, Christianity had grown beyond anything most first-century Christians could have imagined. In the early fourth century, Emperor Constantine famously converted to Christianity and issued the Edict of Milan in 313 AD. This decree ensured tolerance for Christians and offered the church many legal protections that they had never enjoyed.

Several decades after Constantine, an emperor named Julian rose to power. He ruled from 361–63 AD. Julian was raised in the Christian faith but turned away from it as an adult. When he became emperor, he worked to resuscitate the historic polytheistic religion that his ancestors had practiced. Julian did not like the growing influence of Christianity, especially within governmental circles. Christian history would subsequently label Julian "the Apostate," because he walked away from the Christian faith back toward Greco-Roman paganism.

In one of Julian's letters, we find a remarkable statement on Christian influence. Though Julian was antagonistic toward Christianity, he acknowledged how powerful its influence was on the populace. He could see that the public viewed Christian leaders with admiration. Julian wanted pagan priests to adopt that same peculiarly Christian posture so that people would be won back over to the historic Roman religion. In a letter to the pagan high-priest of Galatia, Julian speaks about Christians (whom he snidely calls "atheists" and "Galileans"):

To Arsacius, High-priest of Galatia,

> The Hellenic religion does not yet prosper as I desire . . . why do we not observe that it is their benevolence to strangers, their care for the graves of the dead, and the pretended holiness of their lives that have done the most to increase atheism? I believe that we ought really and truly to practice every one of these virtues. And it is not enough for you alone to practice them, but so must all the priests in Galatia, without exception . . . it is disgraceful that, when no Jew ever has to beg and the impious Galileans support not only their own poor but ours as well, all men should see how our people lack aid from us. Teach those of the Hellenic faith to contribute public service of this sort . . .[1]

How extraordinary that an enemy of Christianity would so openly concede the positive reputation of Christian leaders and the value of their benevolent influence.

What would it look like for Christian influencers to lead in the twenty-first century in such a way that even our most enthusiastic detractors would aspire to follow our example? How would the world change if Christians had such a widely acknowledged reputation for benevolence, as they did in Julian's time?

We have explored in this book many leadership principles that were embraced by Paul and his team. When we step back a little bit further and take a broad view, there appears to have been a handful of bedrock values underlying all of their actions—principles that were so thoroughly embedded in their lives that they're more like personality traits than leadership strategies. Three traits stand out among the rest.

1. Their singular focus was Christ.

We have seen this character trait woven through Paul's experiences and those of his team. It's a rather obvious statement to say that they were passionate about sharing the gospel, but that should not be taken for granted. Many Christians today do not share the same focus on Christ and zeal for evangelism. Paul and his team shared Christ both with people who were enthusiastic listeners and people who were openly hostile to the message. They spoke the name of Jesus to different cultural contexts and in different languages. They made sure not to overburden new believers in ways that might distract from the gospel of grace. They pressed forward with the message of Christ even when—judging by outward appearances—they seemed to be losing badly. Paul vehemently defended the one true gospel when dangerous distortions reared their heads. He knew that distorting the gospel leads to a broken picture of Christ and a skewed view of His work on the cross. Paul's team risked death, imprisonment, and cultural persecution to proclaim the name of Jesus. Christ was the heart of their faith and the driving force of their actions and attitudes. They avoided making their ministry about something—or *someone*—else.

2. They treated others as equals.

Paul and his team valued people and treated them as equals. Everyone is created in God's image, and God loves everyone. We observe this character trait in the actions of Paul's team and, of course, in Paul's writings. When Paul wrote his letters, he told people explicitly that he could not succeed in ministry without them. He made them feel visible and valued, using *syn-* prefix words like "fellow worker" in his letters, which communicated equality. Paul acknowledged he was replaceable by training his successors, and he openly admitted his need for prayer, support, comfort, and refreshment in the personal sections of his letters.

Paul unleashed people for ministry who were new Christians, and he allowed their actions to shape the direction his own ministry took. There was reciprocal influence. Paul railed against disunity when it threatened to break up new congregations, and when given an opportunity to lift someone up, he took it—most notably, casting a vision for Philemon that he should forget about the cultural hierarchy and view Onesimus through God's eyes: as a child of God and thus a brother in Christ.

3. They were agents of reconciliation.

Paul and his team were proactive about reconciliation, working to achieve it before divisions could take root. They sought common ground with people. They built bridges. They were not unnecessarily combative with people who didn't believe what they did. They were thoughtful. They were kind. They did what would stave off the need for reconciliation.

But when division did occur, they worked for reconciliation. They did so in ministry disputes (e.g., Paul and Mark), cultural chasms (e.g., Onesimus and Philemon), and deep hurts inflicted within a close relationship (Paul and the Corinthians). In a broader sense, they were also working for spiritual reconciliation—letting the world know that God loves them and desired so much to be in relationship with humanity that He sent His Son as a means of final reconciliation. Whether it was personal, social, or spiritual reconciliation, Paul and his team worked for it.

Nearly all the lessons we have learned in this book can be fit into one or more of these three traits: a focus on Jesus, a commitment to viewing others as equals, and a commitment to reconciliation. Some fit more neatly than others, but these three basic traits rise to the surface when surveying the terrain we have covered.

ONE FINAL EXAMPLE

There is an important episode in Paul's ministry that we did not yet explore in this book: how the gospel first came to Philippi. It's a fitting way to bring our investigation to a close, because many of the leadership qualities we have observed in

Paul's team are powerfully expressed in Luke's description of what happened (Acts 16:8–40). We can see even more when we pair that with Paul's words in his letter to the Philippians.

To put this era of Paul's ministry into context, Paul first arrived in Philippi in the early 50s AD after traveling from Antioch westward through Asia Minor. When he arrived in Philippi, he probably had Luke, Timothy, and Silas with him. Silas had joined Paul after his split with Barnabas and Mark (Acts 15:40). Timothy joined them when Paul and Silas came through Lystra (Acts 16:1–3). We presume Luke was there because their travel to Philippi is one of the "we" sections in Acts (16:10ff).[2] When they arrived in Philippi in the northern part of Greece, they entered a city that Luke described as "a leading city of the district of Macedonia and a Roman colony" (Acts 16:12). The fact that the city was a Roman colony means that it was settled with Roman citizens and probably included a sizeable contingent of military veterans. On the Sabbath, Luke tells us, Paul and his friends went to a "place of prayer" outside the gate, where they spoke to some women who had gathered there (v. 13). This is another instance of Paul and company seeking common ground, because they were looking to connect with the Jewish community.

Because there is no synagogue mentioned, we can assume that the Jewish population of Philippi was quite small. A synagogue required at least ten Jewish men, and because there was no synagogue mentioned in this text, it is probable that there wasn't one. It seems that there were only a few women in Philippi who worshiped the God of the Jewish Scriptures, and they met by the river to pray on the Sabbath. Paul and his team still viewed this small gathering of Jewish women to be worth their initial effort; they were just as valuable to God.

One of the women there was named Lydia, who, according to Luke, sold "purple goods" (Acts 16:14). This indicates that she was wealthy, because she worked in a lucrative niche of the textile industry. God spoke to her through Paul's words, and she placed her faith in Christ—the first convert to Christianity in Europe. She invited Paul's team to stay at her home, another indication of her wealth (v. 15).

Soon afterwards, a slave girl who had been possessed by a spirit of divination annoyed Paul so greatly by following him around that he cast out the demon (Acts 16:18). Because her owners made money off of her fortune-telling skills, they hauled Paul and Silas before the rulers in the marketplace (v. 19). "'These men are Jews, and they are disturbing our city,'" they claimed (v. 20). This was clearly an anti-Semitic statement, proven by the fact that they only brought Paul and Silas (who were Jewish) before the magistrates.[3] Paul and Silas were beaten and thrown into prison (v. 23). They definitely seemed to be losing at this point.

That evening, while in prison, Paul and Silas demonstrated a clear reliance on God by praying and singing hymns. An earthquake shook the prison and released them, which led to an opportunity to share Christ with the jailer. He asked them, "What must I do to be saved?" (Acts 16:30). Paul's answer was Christ-centered and burden-free: "Believe in the Lord Jesus, and you will be saved, you and your household" (v. 31). He and his family were baptized (v. 33).

When the magistrates commanded the jailer to release Paul and Silas, Paul replied, "They have beaten us publicly, uncondemned, men who are Roman citizens, and have thrown us into prison; and do they now throw us out secretly? No! Let them come themselves and take us out" (Acts 16:37). It was a significant benefit for Paul and Silas to be Roman citizens, and in this case they used their citizenship to hold the governmental authorities accountable for their wrongful imprisonment. The goal, however, was not simply to embarrass the leaders. Scholars debate what the purpose was for Paul's insistence on an apology, but it may have been to provide some level of legitimacy and protection for the brand-new Christian community that included Lydia and the jailer, especially since Paul and company intended to leave soon. After receiving the apology from the Philippian magistrates, they were asked to leave the city (v. 39).

About a decade later, Paul wrote a letter from his Roman jail cell to the Philippian Christians, the very same community that started out with Lydia and the jailer. He wrote eloquently about his affection and thankfulness for the Philippians: "I thank my God in all my remembrance of you, always in every prayer of mine for you all making my prayer with joy, because of your partnership in the gospel from the first day until now" (Phil. 1:3–5).

Paul sees God at work in their lives, and he wants to encourage the Philippian Christians to press forward and continue to grow in their relationship with Christ. As Paul continues his letter, we see him encouraging the Philippians to adopt some of the same personality traits we have observed in Paul's team:

> complete my joy by being of the same mind, having the same love, being in full accord and of one mind.

> Do nothing from selfish ambition or conceit, but
> in humility count others more significant than
> yourselves. Let each of you look not only to his own
> interests, but also to the interests of others. Have this
> mind among yourselves, which is yours in Christ
> Jesus. (Phil. 2:2–5)

Familiar themes abound here, such as unity, peace, and viewing others as your equal (or in this case—as *more* significant than yourself!). But *why* do we act this way? How is it even possible to live this way?

Paul answers in the very next verses; we look to Christ as our example:

> [Christ Jesus,] who, though he was in the form of
> God, did not count equality with God a thing to be
> grasped, but emptied himself, by taking the form of
> a servant, being born in the likeness of men. And
> being found in human form, he humbled himself by
> becoming obedient to the point of death, even death
> on a cross. Therefore God has highly exalted him
> and bestowed on him the name that is above every
> name, so that at the name of Jesus every knee should
> bow, in heaven and on earth and under the earth, and
> every tongue confess that Jesus Christ is Lord, to the
> glory of God the Father. (Phil. 2:6–11)

There again is that singular focus on Christ. Everything we do is a reflection of what He has already done for us. On the cross, Christ humbled Himself and became the definitive agent of reconciliation.

In his letters, Paul applies these truths in particular ways to specific situations. For example, he applies our unity in Christ to a division he knows exists between two specific Christians in Philippi:

> I entreat Euodia and I entreat Syntyche to agree in the Lord. Yes, I ask you also, true companion, help these women, who have labored side by side with me in the gospel together with Clement and the rest of my fellow workers, whose names are in the book of life.
>
> Rejoice in the Lord always; again I will say, rejoice. Let your reasonableness be known to everyone. The Lord is at hand. (Phil. 4:2–5)

Paul encourages the Philippians to let their *reasonableness* be known. The word he uses there could also be translated as "gentleness," "forbearance," or "graciousness."[4] We Christians are envoys of truth and reconciliation, and this should be seen not only in our relationships with one another, but in our conduct with "everyone" (v. 5). We must not see ourselves as at war with outsiders, but as agents of God's peace, loving those whom He loves yet who are far from Christ.

As Christians, we seek common ground. We watch the burdens we place on people that distract from Christ. We empower people to lead. We revive broken relationships. We fight the battles that actually matter. We partner with people for God's purposes. We build bridges across cultural chasms. We steward relationships. We make people feel visible and valued. We are relentless about restoration. We keep going when we feel like we're losing. We admit we're replaceable. We focus on Christ, value others, and work for reconciliation in whatever ways we can. This is the distinctively Christian brand of influence, our peculiar posture as leaders. This is our way.

Now it is time for you to seek the Lord's guidance on how to embody the personality traits we have observed in Paul's team. It's time to begin praying that God would use your influence for His purposes, whatever that influence might be. We have an excellent example to follow in Paul's team, and now we must acknowledge and embrace our roles as influencers. We must set examples for others, because they will one day serve as examples for others, who will set examples for others, and so on.

When we feel unsure about our leadership and influence, we can rediscover our purpose and identity by looking to Christ. When we're unsure how that purpose should play out in our daily lives, we can look to Paul and his team. Their example is always available to us.

Having now looked closely at Paul and his team, I can think of no better concluding words than some of Paul's to the Philippians: "What you have learned and received and heard and seen in me—practice these things, and the God of peace will be with you" (Phil. 4:9).

QUESTIONS FOR DISCUSSION/REFLECTION

- What stood out to you about this chapter?
- What did you find most challenging about this chapter?
- What did you find most surprising about this book?

- How have the actions of Paul and his team changed your view toward leadership and influence?
- What is your biggest takeaway from this book?
- What practical step can you take in the next few weeks to conform your influence to what you observed in Paul's team?
- Sample Prayer: Heavenly Father, help the example of Paul and his team to stick with me. Help it to settle down into my heart and influence the way I influence others. I want to lead well in the sphere of influence You have given me, and I need Your help to do that. Lord, I want to reach the end of my life, as Paul did, feeling that I had run the race well—not perfectly, but well, relying on You and trusting You for guidance. Please help that to be true of me, and show me the path to get there. Amen.

Notes

Introduction

1. It is beyond the scope of this book to cover every known member of Paul's team, and some will receive more attention than others. I will also not be able to address leadership examples from every locale that Paul visited.

2. Much of what I will write is based on the basic biblical and theological knowledge required to earn a seminary degree and a university PhD. That being the case, I will not exhaustively provide a citation for every piece of information that is drawn from that general knowledge base I gained in my education. I will note any specific source—ancient or modern—that I reference, quote, or otherwise draw upon.

3. Adapted from Map 106, "The Jewish Diaspora at Pentecost," in Barry J. Beitzel, *The New Moody Atlas of the Bible* (Chicago: Moody, 2009), 250.

Chapter One: The Quest for Common Ground

1. F. F. Bruce, *Paul: Apostle of the Heart Set Free* (Grand Rapids: Eerdmans, 2000), 33–36.

2. There is ancient evidence outside of the New Testament for the existence of altars like this in Athens. See Pausanius, *Description of Greece*, 1.1.4.

3. Epimenides and Aratus

4. Paul used the verb δουλόω (*douloō*), which means, "to make one a slave." M. Zerwick and M. Grosvenor, *A Grammatical Analysis of the Greek New Testament* (Rome: Gregorian and Biblical Press, 2013), 515.

Chapter Two: Watch the Burden

1. Bruce, *Paul*, 475. Throughout this book I will follow F. F. Bruce's chronology, which is reflective of generally accepted timelines for Paul's ministry career.

2. Barclay Newman, *Greek-English Dictionary* in *The UBS Greek New Testament, A Reader's Edition* (Stuttgart: Deutsche Bibelgesellschaft, 2007), 357.

Chapter Three: Offstage Leadership

1. Susan Cain, *Quiet: The Power of Introverts in a World That Can't Stop Talking* (New York: Crown Publishers, 2012).

2. In Paul's ministry there were several examples of prominent women responding early to the gospel in places like Thessalonica (Acts 17:4), Berea (Acts 17:12), and Philippi (Acts 16:14).

3. Other ancient sources that address Luke's biography and ministry include: The Muratorian Fragment; Anti-Marcionite Prologue to Luke; Irenaeus's *Against Heresies* 3.1; Eusebius's *The Church History* 3.4; 3.24.

Chapter Four: More Than a Ceasefire

1. Joseph Ellis, *Founding Brothers: The Revolutionary Generation* (New York: Vintage Books, 2000), 164.
2. Benjamin Rush to John Adams. February 17, 1812 (founders.archives.gov).
3. Ellis, *Founding Brothers*, 230.
4. J. P. Louw and E.A. Nida, *Greek-English Lexicon of the New Testament Based on Semantic Domains, 2nd Edition* (New York: United Bible Societies, 1988), 33.451.
5. M. Zerwick and M. Grosvenor, *A Grammatical Analysis of the Greek New Testament* (Rome: Gregorian and Biblical Press, 2013), 403.
6. Paul mentions Barnabas in 1 Corinthians 9:6; Galatians 2:1, 9, 13; and Colossians 4:10.
7. On Mark's authorship of the gospel see also Eusebius's *Ecclesiastical History* 2.15, 3.39 and 6.14; the Anti-Marcionite Prologue to Mark; the Muratorian Fragment; Irenaeus's *Against Heresies* 3.1; and Tertullian's *Against Marcion* 4.5.

Chapter Five: Worthy Conflicts

1. Donald T. Phillips, *Lincoln on Leadership: Executive Strategies for Tough Times* (New York: Grand Central Publishing, 1992), 70.
2. Ibid., 66.
3. Some key gospel texts include John 3:16; Romans 3:23; 5:8; 6:23; 10:9; Ephesians 2:4–9; 2 Corinthians 5:17–21; and Titus 3:3–7.
4. Phillips, *Lincoln on Leadership*, 74.

Chapter Six: Genuine Collaboration

1. Josephus, *The Jewish War*, 3:540.
2. Suetonius, *Life of Claudius*, 25.4. Translated by Catharine Edwards in *Lives of the Caesars*, Oxford World's Classics (Oxford: Oxford University Press, 2000), 184.
3. The Greek word is μένω (*menō*). It is used, for example, to describe when Mary stayed with Elizabeth for three months during her pregnancy (Luke 1:56). See also Luke 8:27; 9:4; 10:7; 19:5; 24:29; and Acts 9:43; 16:15; 18:20; 21:7–8; 28:16.
4. According to F. F. Bruce, this is "in line with [Paul's] habit of referring to people by their formal names (in his letters, at any rate); Luke refers to them by their more familiar names. Thus Paul says Silvanus where Luke says Silas; Paul says Sosipater where Luke says Sopater." F. F. Bruce, *The Pauline Circle* (Eugene, OR: Wipf and Stock Publishers, 2006), 45.
5. M. Zerwick and M. Grosvenor, *A Grammatical Analysis of the Greek New Testament* (Rome: Gregorian and Biblical Press, 2013), 496.
6. Barclay Newman, *Greek-English Dictionary in The UBS Greek New Testament, A Reader's Edition* (Stuttgart: Deutsche Bibelgesellshaft, 2007), 687.
7. By the mid-60s, Erastus was back at home in Corinth, according to Paul's final letter: "Erastus remained at Corinth, and I left Trophimus, who was ill, at Miletus" (2 Tim. 4:20).

8. Another notable example would be the Pontius Pilate inscription discovered at Caesarea Maritima.

9. Everett Ferguson, *Backgrounds of Early Christianity*, 3rd Edition (Grand Rapids: Eerdmans Publishing Co., 2003), 42. Latin text of the inscription: ERASTUS PRO AEDILITATE S. P. STRAVIT.

10. Ibid.

11. In Acts 19:31, we discover that Paul was also friends with some local government officials in Ephesus.

Chapter Seven: Kingdom Diplomacy

1. Ryan Lokkesmoe, "Finding Onesimus: Recovering the Story of a First-Century Fugitive Slave," PhD diss., University of Denver, 2015), 125. Unless otherwise specified, the information in this chapter is drawn from my dissertation, which can be accessed via ProQuest (project number 3731228) through the University of Denver Library (library.du.edu).

2. Ibid, 129–30.

3. In my dissertation, I argued against the theory that Onesimus left Philemon's home with the premeditated intention of enlisting Paul's help (the so-called *Amicus Domini* theory). I argued instead that Onesimus fled with no intention of ever returning, but decided at some point to seek out the apostle long after the fact. I call this modified theory *Amicus Domini Ex Post Facto*, and I believe it takes the best stock of the historical, textual, archaeological, legal, and rhetorical evidence.

4. Everett Ferguson, *Backgrounds of Early Christianity*, 3rd Edition (Grand Rapids: Eerdmans Publishing Co., 2003), 562. See also Josephus, *The Jewish War*, 5.193–194; 6.124–126; *Antiquities of the Jews*. 15.417.

5. There was a bishop of Ephesus named Onesimus in the early second century. It is not certain that this bishop was the same Onesimus as the man in Paul's letter. Paul probably wrote the letter to Philemon sometime in the early 60s AD, and this Onesimus served as Bishop of Ephesus about four decades later. If it was the same man, he would have been very young during the time of Paul's letter and relatively old when serving as a bishop. It's not impossible, but it's improbable. If the bishop was the young fugitive in Paul's letter, it is possible that he kept the letter because of its personal significance for him, especially if he gained his freedom because of it. Ignatius mentioned this Onesimus in a letter he wrote to the Ephesians around Trajan's reign in the early second century. In that letter, Ignatius wrote, "Since, therefore, I have received in God's name your whole congregation in the person of Onesimus, a man of inexpressible love who is also your earthly bishop, I pray that you will love him in accordance with the standard set by Jesus Christ and that all of you will be like him. For blessed is the one who has graciously allowed you, worthy as you are, to have such a bishop." Ignatius, *Epistle to the Ephesians* 1.3, in *The Apostolic Fathers, 3rd Edition,* ed. and trans. Michael W. Holmes (Grand Rapids: Baker Academic, 2007), 170.

Chapter Eight: Relational Stewardship

1. Adapted from James P. Ware, *Synopsis of the Pauline Letters in Greek and English* (Grand Rapids: Baker Academic, 2010), xxix.
2. Michael Thompson, "The Holy Internet: Communication between Churches in the First Christian Generation," in *The Gospels for All Christians: Rethinking the Gospel Audiences*, ed. Richard Bauckham et. al (Grand Rapids: W.B. Eerdmans, 1998), 56–58.
3. In several instances, Paul notes when he is writing a portion of the letter in his own hand. "I, Paul, write this greeting with my own hand" (1 Cor. 16:21); "See with what large letters I am writing to you with my own hand" (Gal. 6:11); "I, Paul, write this greeting with my own hand" (Col. 4:18); "I, Paul, write this greeting with my own hand. This is the sign of genuineness in every letter of mine; it is the way I write" (2 Thess. 3:17); "I, Paul, write this with my own hand" (Philem. 19).
4. It is true that in some letters Paul emphasized his apostolic status and defended his right to leadership, but those were in contexts where his legitimacy had been challenged (e.g., Galatians, 2 Corinthians).

Chapter Nine: Relentless About Reconciliation

1. For more info, see Ryan Lokkesmoe, "Titus," in the *Lexham Bible Dictionary*, eds. J. D. Barry and L. Wentz (Bellingham, WA: Lexham Press, 2012). Electronic edition.
2. Frederick W. Danker, et al., *A Greek-English Lexicon of the New Testament and Other Early Christian Literature* (Chicago: University of Chicago Press, 2000), 521. The related Greek word ἀλλάσσω (*allássō*) means "to make something other or different, change, alter, exchange" (ibid., 45–46). This is the same connotation as the word Paul used for reconciliation (καταλλάσσω, *katallassō*), just without the relational dimension.
3. C. S. Lewis, *The Screwtape Letters* (reprint, New York: HarperOne, 2001), 28.

Chapter Ten: Trust in the Fog

1. For more on the growth of global Christianity, see Wes Granberg-Michaelson's article in the *Washington Post* titled "Think Christianity is dying? No, Christianity is shifting dramatically" (May 20, 2015). See also Mark Noll's excellent volume, *The New Shape of World Christianity* (Downers Grove, IL: InterVarsity Press, 2009).
2. Ovid, *Metamorphoses* 8.626–724.
3. In Philippians 2:19–22, Paul had this to say about Timothy: "I hope in the Lord Jesus to send Timothy to you soon, so that I too may be cheered by news of you. For I have no one like him, who will be genuinely concerned for your welfare. For they all seek their own interests, not those of Jesus Christ. But you know Timothy's proven worth, how as a son with a father he has served with me in the gospel."
4. *Lexham Bible Dictionary*, eds. J. D. Barry and L. Wentz (Bellingham, WA: Lexham Press, 2012). Electronic edition.

Chapter Eleven: Fade to the Background

1. You can read the writings of these second generation Christian leaders in the ancient texts known collectively as *The Apostolic Fathers*.
2. Kate Shellnutt, "Only 1 in 7 Senior Pastors is Under 40", *Christianity Today*, January 26, 2017.
3. Tacitus, *Annals of Imperial Rome*, 15.38ff.
4. Ibid., 15.44.
5. Pliny, *Letters* 10.96, in *The Letters of the Younger Pliny,* trans. Betty Radice (London: Penguin Books, 1969), 293–95.
6. *The Apostolic Fathers: Greek Texts and English Translations, 3rd Edition,* ed. and trans. Michael W. Holmes (Grand Rapids: Baker Academic, 2007), 33–43.
7. Ibid., 109.

Conclusion

1. Ramsey MacMullen and Eugene N. Lane, eds., *Paganism and Christianity, 100–425 C.E.* (Minneapolis: Augsburg Fortress, 1992), 270–71.
2. Paul mentions Silas a handful of times in his letters, using the more formal version of his name, Silvanus (2 Cor. 1:19; 1 Thess. 1:1; 2 Thess. 1:1). Silvanus is listed with Paul and Timothy as a co-sender of both Thessalonian letters. This supports Luke's narrative in Acts that puts Silas and Timothy with Paul during his journey southward from Philippi toward Thessalonica, Athens, and Corinth (Acts 16–18).
3. According to early-church traditions, Luke was a Gentile exchange" (see note 3 in chapter 3 above). Timothy was only half-Jewish and raised in a Gentile environment (Acts 16:1–3).
4. J. P. Louw and E.A. Nida, *Greek-English Lexicon of the New Testament Based on Semantic Domains, 2nd Edition* (New York: United Bible Societies, 1988), 88.63.

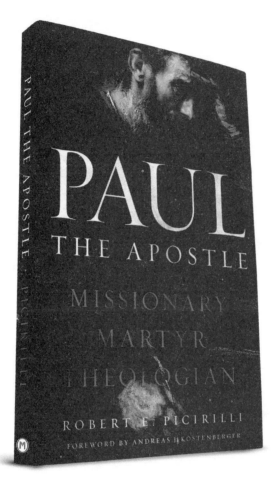

ere are two styles of leadership
at war in the world

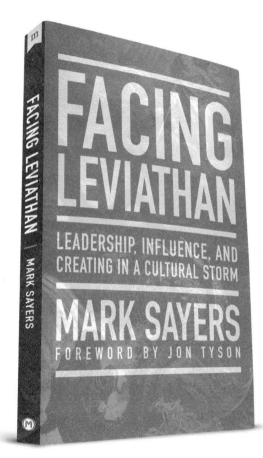

Revive your leadership.
Grow healthy teams.
See great results.

For more information visit:

rareleadership.net